Take Charge of Your Health Care Career: Successful Job-Search Strategies for the Health Care Professional

Written by:

Hal Patterson, MPA

Published by:
Medical Group Management Association
104 Inverness Terrace East
Englewood CO 80112
(303) 799-1111

Medical Group Management Association (MGMA) publications are intended to provide current and accurate information and are designed to assist readers in becoming more familiar with the subject matter covered. Such publications are distributed with the understanding that MGMA does not render any legal, accounting or other professional advice that may be construed as specifically applicable to individual situations. No representation or warranties are made concerning the application of legal or other principles discussed by the author to any specific factual situation, nor is any prediction made concerning how any particular judge, government official or other person will interpret or apply such principles. Specific factual situations should be discussed with professional advisors.

MEDICAL GROUP
MANAGEMENT
ASSOCIATION

© 1998 Hal Patterson, MPA

Medical Group Management Association
104 Inverness Terrace East
Englewood CO 80112

ISBN # 1-56829-089-6
Item # 5142

Table of Contents

Chapter 7: Take charge of your negotiation. **267**

Appendix 1: Some recommended references and resources . . . **287**

Appendix 2: A review of the important ideas and techniques. . **291**

Acknowledgments

I owe much to Dr. Perry Luckett for his valuable ideas on persuasion, which underlie my treatment of resumes and cover letters, as well as for his help in editing all drafts of the manuscript.

I'm also grateful to the many clients within the Medical Group Management Association and the Healthcare Financial Management Association who have provided the basis for most of the examples used in this book. In fact, they inspired this book. Their hard work and success in using the concepts described in the book motivated me to write it.

Thanks also for the support provided by Cynthia Kiyotake, MA, MGMA Library Resource Director and her staff, as well as the book production assistance of Discovery Communications, Inc., Network Graphics and Huey Desktop Publishing.

About the author

Hal Patterson, MPA, President of Patterson Enterprises, an organization development and career planning company in Denver, CO, has more than 23 years of experience helping organizations and individuals succeed by designing and implementing career development and organization development projects. Hal has consulted with organizations on the design and implementation of career planning systems, and has designed and conducted career planning and job-search skill programs for individuals. He received his bachelor's and master's degrees in human resources and organizational development at the University of Colorado-Boulder.

Hal developed the Career Resource Service for the Medical Group Management Association (MGMA) and has helped the Healthcare Financial Management Association (HFMA) develop a career resource service for its members. He conducts career planning workshops for various MGMA state organizations, and works with MGMA and HFMA members on personalized career planning and job-search skill programs.

He has authored *Mapping Your Career: A Working Guide for Health Care Professionals,* a manual used in conjunction with MGMA career continuation workshops and one-on-one counseling sessions. In addition, Hal authors career planning articles for the *MGM Update* newspaper as well as for other publications.

Chapter 1

Why should I read this book?

You may be saying, "Oh great, here's another book on job search skills." So why is this one any different from the other 500 already on bookstore shelves or the one on my shelf?

NOTES

- It's based on my years of experience helping medical group administrators, managers, chief financial officers, nurses and physicians struggle with career-related decisions as health care changes around them;

- It takes a surprisingly simple and practical approach to planning for and doing an effective job search. I know of many medical managers who were getting literally no responses to their traditional methods of using a resume. After talking to me about ways to "repackage" themselves, the phone began ringing to schedule interviews; and

- I believe this is the first book to look freshly at how to market yourself in the world of mergers, affiliations, integrations and downsizings – today's health care world.

This book is for you if you truly want to take a practical, effective approach to searching for a job. Although the focus and most examples are health-care related, the techniques and principles apply to everyone, if you're thinking about changing jobs, in any profession, or if you've recently experienced a downsizing and must look for another job.

I've worked with materials from various career-planning and outplacement approaches. After using several different approaches, I've learned there is no BEST way to plan for and carry out a

job search. In fact, every BEST approach has two or three counter suggestions. I'm sure 10 career consultants or job-search experts would give you at least 15 ways to search for a job.

But **the tips and techniques described in this book work**. I've helped hundreds of clients develop plans that led to successful job searches. And I've counseled individual clients to think about and complete detailed career plans — to take charge of their careers and job searches. I know numerous reference guides are on the market today that say they contain "the latest trends and ideas in job-search techniques." I've consolidated many of these ideas and added the most successful techniques I know to create a succinct, yet successful approach to finding that ideal job.

How does this book help me manage change?

By focusing on a vital theme for your future — take control of your career. This means being career resilient. Gone are the days when you could trade your loyalty to an employer and hard work for job security and steady promotions. You can't depend on (or expect) your organization, large or small, to manage your career for you. Instead, you must manage your own career — a responsibility that requires much of you.

It begins by planning for and having a career "check-up" — stepping back, at least once a year, and reflecting on what subtle changes are taking place around you. Have you heard rumors of a merger or integration with another organization that you've conveniently ignored or decided won't affect you? Have your job responsibilities changed? Are you asked to take on new tasks that don't motivate? Has the mission of your organization changed? Have you clearly defined your "purpose" or "mission"? You need to continually assess your situation, skills, personal needs and work commitments so you're empowered to make decisions that result in satisfying work and increase your motivation and energy. You must upgrade your skills so you're "marketable" in the future. In addition:

- Be continually alert to how your values match the changing environment, which may affect your energy, commitment and motivation. This is especially true for physicians and nurses. Changes in health care are creating major internal conflict for some physicians and nurses because decisions about patient care is being passed to third parties, such as insurance companies;

- Recognize the effect on you if the organization you work for becomes part of an integrated system. It's easy for you to assume that, because your job didn't change (or you even received a promotion), everything will remain the same. Chances are it won't! New ownership or management will always create different operating philosophies you may not agree with;

- If you're not happy with your situation, determine what you need to change in your current work and environment, and act;

- If you're not sure what and where you can contribute in the future, define your personal mission (your purpose) and career goals — then develop and carry out a career action plan. The most successful people are those who find their own career paths instead of the path outside influences lay out for them;

- If you identify skills you need to develop or enhance, create a personal-development plan and follow through. But remember, the new skills you are developing today will be outdated within two to three years, maybe sooner. The process continues;

NOTES

- Keep your resume up to date. Highlight accomplishments and achievements monthly; otherwise, you may forget what you did (accomplished). Keep a running list of accomplishments and use them to prove your value to your current (and future) employers;

- Anticipate and expect change. Prepare for the unexpected. Plan now; and

- Recognize that re-alignments, downsizings, mergers and acquisitions will always directly affect you and your career.

How does this book help me take control of my career?

It helps you understand that taking control of your career and the decisions that affect it begins with identifying your personal mission and then diligently planning to move toward it – create your personal career plan.

What does career planning have to do with job-search strategies. My response: a lot — for two key reasons.

First, identifying your values, interests, skills, accomplishments and ideal environment means you can base your decisions on data, not emotion — or worse, desperation.

Take Control

- Identify your values, interests, skills, accomplishments, ideal environment.

- Identify your mission and career-goal alternatives.

Second, identifying your mission and career-goal alternatives prepares you to select and rank job opportunities; you're more qualified to assess how well a particular job "matches" your preferences. If you perceive a match, you can confidently work hard to get an offer. If you perceive little or no match, you can confidently move on to other opportunities while wasting no time and energy.

I have one example in which this evaluation was painful, yet positive, for a client. My client was a recent graduate of a Master's in Health

4

Administration program but was unclear as to the type of medical environment she wanted to work in. Her conclusion after completing her career plan was surprising, yet one she had suspected for some time: she didn't want a job in health care. This was indeed a startling conclusion for someone who had just completed her master's course work and internship. The good news? She identified other environments that did motivate, then concentrated her job search and self-marketing efforts in those areas. Yes, her master's degree applied. Without taking the time to do career planning, she might have pursued a job in health care while feeling something was wrong but not exactly sure why.

How will I learn to take control?

You'll learn specific strategies and techniques to:

1) Prepare yourself to take control of your job search;

2) Identify key parts of your self-marketing portfolio;

3) Develop your resume database, which you'll use to customize cover letters and resumes, prepare marketing letters, and plan for and conduct interviews confidently and competently;

4) Research ways to meet the needs (requirements) of the hiring organization — at every step in the job search;

5) Show how your experiences, background and accomplishments MATCH an organization's needs, qualifications and requirements;

6) Put your needs and requirements "on the back burner" during the search, at least until the second and third interview;

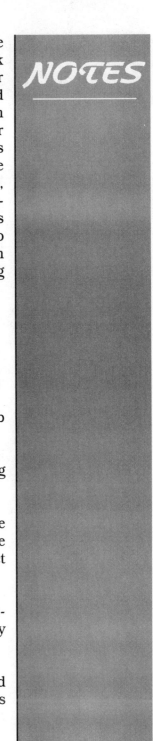

7) Negotiate a final offer that successfully meets your requirements, as well as the hiring organization's needs; and

8) Suggest and write employment contracts that protect you and the hiring organization.

What if I have other ideas or questions about my job search?

In this book, I'll try to stimulate your thinking about ways to improve your search for that perfect job. If you've used a technique I don't describe, I'd love to hear about it, how it worked, and the outcomes. Please write, fax, e-mail, or use the old-fashioned telephone to tell me about your success:

Mail:	Hal Patterson 3038 S. Gilpin Street Denver, CO 80210
Phone:	(303) 692-9588
Fax:	(303) 692-0034
E-mail:	hp3038@concentric.net

Also, if you try any of these techniques and they don't work, I'd like to hear about it. We could review what you did, how it worked, and jointly come up with a different approach. One thing is certain about job search – every situation is unique. We all need to keep working toward successful strategies that we can apply correctly.

Good luck and happy job hunting!

Chapter 2

Take charge of your career

In this chapter, we'll set the stage for planning and doing a successful job search by first discussing how you can take control of your career. Then we'll identify the prevalent barriers to managing your career. Finally, I will introduce you to five active strategies for managing your career.

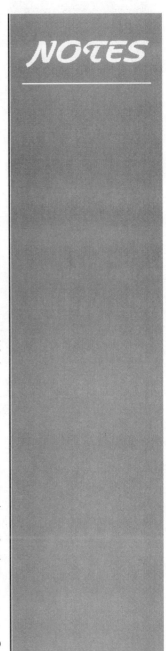

Why take control of my career?

During the planning and research for this book, a colleague asked why I was writing it. The reason is my theme — *Take Charge* — not only of your job search but also of your career and all decisions that affect it. I want to help you recognize that you must control your career, which means you must plan for and do your job search with the same sense of control. Recognize you can use various techniques and strategies to direct your search, rather than allowing the decision-making control to come from others — search firms, placement services, hiring organizations, etc. To take control means to be *career self-reliant*. You must rely on your plans, actions and decisions — not those of others.

To be successful in today's health care environment, you must plan where and how you will work. Suppose you lost your job tomorrow because of a layoff caused by something outside your control, such as an integration, merger or acquisition? It's unlikely you have a well-thought-out, updated career plan or a complete strategy. If you're like 95 percent of the workforce, you spend more time planning your holiday parties and vacations than planning your career. This is a sobering thought, especially today, when the work world is changing so rapidly around us.

Why is career planning important? Health care faces market, competitive and environmental pressures as never before. Change affects jobs. Ask yourself: "How has my job changed over the past 12 months? How might it change in the next 12 months? What can I do now to anticipate these changes? Will any changes directly affect my job? Will I be forced to find another job soon, allowing others to make decisions about my job for me?"

We usually let organizations make decisions about our careers with little or no input from us. That's because we get caught up in an outdated paradigm when we think about work. We still view work and our job the way our parents and grandparents did. Remember how loyal and committed they were to their work and their companies?

Loyalty and commitment were rewarded because companies provided life-long employment. Layoffs and downsizing didn't happen. Companies took care of workers and their careers through logical and planned promotions. Moving up within the company was automatic. Companies encouraged promotions by providing access to professional development and training that supported a well-defined career path.   An implicit contract existed between employee and the company — if you worked hard and did a good job, you could count on a job until retirement.

It's different today! And most of us aren't prepared for these differences. Look around, how have your environment and daily responsibilities changed? Has the implicit contract that used to exist between you and your employer changed or disappeared?

Faced with such dramatic change, organizations have all but scuttled loyalty and commitment. They now make decisions based on bottom-line results, even if that means downsizing and layoffs. That means you must be in charge of your career. Decide what you will do and be; don't let others decide for you.

I have worked with many people whose medical group was integrated into a larger health care network, after which corporate officers decided on staffing. What if you're part of an integration this year? Decisions will be made for you, often without your input or opinion. You may be offered a position or you may not. If you are offered a position, it may not meet your needs or match your skills and interests.

What are the obstacles to managing my career?

To manage your own career, ask yourself: What are the obstacles I face? How can I best overcome them to take control? Five typical obstacles are:

- Procrastination;
- Fear of change;
- Reluctance to give up what you have and know;
- Lack of knowledge about yourself; and
- Lack of personal career planning and goal-setting.

Procrastination

It's easy to put off until tomorrow what you could be doing today, even when it concerns your career and job search. I often hear: "I'll wait until after the holidays; besides, I'm overloaded with year-end administrative work." Then, soon after the new year, I hear: "I'm exhausted having just survived the holidays and year-end closing. I think I need time to rest and get myself organized." Before you know it, summer is here and you're planning your summer vacation and then dealing with end-of-school activities. Before long, 12 months have passed and you haven't found the time to think about your own career and determine if it's moving in the appropriate direction. Instead you put it off and say, "Oh well, I'll get to it next year!" The cycle continues.

NOTES

Fear of change

Change means losing something you know and find comfortable. Change implies a new beginning, and a new beginning implies something unknown. Unfortunately, we usually fear the unknown — especially when it applies to careers. Thus, you may wait for decisions to be made for you.

I worked for an organization where more than 85 percent of the staff didn't like their jobs or their bosses, but (and this is the interesting part) not one person left voluntarily. Not one person planned and carried out a move to an organization and job that better matched his or her needs. Even though the company was downsizing (60 percent of the staff was downsized over four years), people stayed — waiting and hoping they wouldn't be caught. All had their reasons — the common theme I heard was, "It would take effort and time on my part to find another job, and besides, this downsizing won't affect me." People seemed paralyzed; they were resigned to staying with the status quo even though their jobs and the environment were very unpleasant.

But what actually happened? I've kept in touch with most of those who were laid off. They all found better jobs in environments that more closely matched their personal preferences — 100 percent! All wondered why they didn't make the move earlier — why they would "stick with" a situation that was so unpleasant.

Lack of information about yourself

I'm continually struck by how few people can accurately describe and confidently discuss themselves: their values, interests, preferences, skills. I'm also struck by the responses I get when I ask if they can describe their personal "mission." Although people can very succinctly describe what they can't do or don't like to do, most stutter and seem confused by my question. A common response: "How would I know!" Or, "I suppose it's what I've always done." Whenever I ask this question in one-on-one sessions for career planning or initial sessions to outline job-search strategies, I usually hear general comments such as "I like working with people," or "I like solving problems." Sometimes I hear, "I guess I've never thought about it before." Have you heard yourself use statements like these? This isn't a strong way to begin a job search.

Lack of planning and personal goal-setting

Fewer than five percent of health care executives have developed and are using a well-thought-out, yet flexible, career plan. Do you have one? If you do, don't stop reading. You should review and update it. If you don't, begin developing one now. Career and job planning seems foreign to most people. Surprised? I pointed out earlier that you will probably spend more time arranging holiday parties and family vacations than planning for your career. Career planning is usually a low priority and may be completely ignored, even though health care is moving quickly toward fewer traditional jobs and more untraditional career opportunities.

What techniques can I use to take charge?

You can actively manage and take control of your career by using five key techniques:

1. Update your education and training;
2. Think "project," not job;
3. Add value to the organization;
4. Develop a short-term plan for contingencies; and
5. Develop a long-term career plan and objectives:
   • Discover your career self;
   • Define your career goal(s); and
   • Develop your career plan(s).

Key Techniques

• Update education, training.
• Think "project," not job.
• Add value to organization.
• Develop short-term contingency plan
• Develop long-term career plan and objectives

Update your education and training – continually

You must update your skills and acquire new ones to remain competitive and employable, especially if you hope to remain with the same organization. Some studies show that our current skills and knowledge become outdated every 18 months because technology advances and the organization's needs change with customer's demands.

Think "project," not job

Think about your job in terms of projects, not as long-term employment in that job or organization. Project or contract work may be the work of the future as working full time until retirement becomes less likely.

In Job Shift — How to Prosper in a Workplace Without Jobs, William Bridges suggests that as employment rises in this country, the number of good, steady jobs continues to decline. He states: "Many people work as temporary or contingent employees. Companies assign tasks to consultants and free-lancers, or outsource them. The vision of a job that we grew up with — the 9 to 5 workday, 12 months a year, with promotions and a pension at age 65 — seems to be vanishing." [1]

Look around your organization. What work is now outsourced to other companies that traditionally had been handled within? Are there parts of your job that are now outsourced? You may be surprised.

Add value to the organization

You must justify your existence by being able to show that you improve your organization's bottom line in some way. Maybe it's providing income or

---

[1] Job Shift: How to Prosper in a Workplace Without Jobs, William Bridges; Addison-Wesley; 1994.

profit by cutting operating expenses, suggesting some efficient ways to do business, improving customer service, or acquiring new customers and generating new revenue. If you demonstrate and communicate your achievements, you should be in a more powerful position during a merger or integration.

Here's one technique. Keep a detailed and updated list of all your completed projects and accomplishments. Describe what you did, the individual actions you took, and any specific results. Communicate these to your immediate supervisor. Contrary to what you may have been told when growing up, it's OK to "toot your own horn." Continually update this list — chances are you have already forgotten projects or assignments you completed six months ago. Do you remember every project you completed five years ago? Seven years ago? Probably not.

Develop a short-term plan for contingencies

Be prepared to act immediately and confidently if you were to lose your job tomorrow. We don't like to think about losing our jobs. But I've consulted with many people who have. In each situation, they ignored the warning signs. To develop a short-term plan or strategy, ask yourself these questions:

1. How has the environment in which I work changed? List the major changes and state whether the changes are positive or negative.

2. What aspects of my job have changed over the past 18 months? (Check as many as apply.)

    ❑ Objectives and goals of the group practice or hospital
    ❑ Personal duties and responsibilities
    ❑ Pressure to increase market share
    ❑ Reimbursement changes
    ❑ Growing overhead and pressure to increase revenues

NOTES

❑ Competition for patients among health care providers

❑ Hours I spend at the group practice

❑ Government regulations or other regulatory changes

❑ Others (list below):

3. How might my job change in the next 18 months? List your ideas:

4. Thinking about the people who have expectations of me within the group practice, for example, the physicians, staff, patients and vendors:

   a: How have their expectations changed?

   b: How might their expectations change in the future?

5. Have I heard rumors of mergers or affiliations that could change my position within the group or hospital?
   ❑ Yes   ❑ No

6. Can I clearly discuss the question "Who am I?" in three minutes to someone I don't know?
   ❑ Yes   ❑ No

In either case, can I complete the following statements:

In both my personal and professional life, I **VALUE:** (e.g., helping others, helping society, achieving goals)

My personal and professional **INTERESTS** are: (e.g., continue my education, advancing in my job)

Things I know **I CAN DO**, and would like to do, in the future are: (e.g., use my skills in computers; finance or accounting skills; managing people)

The **CONDITIONS** or **ENVIRONMENT** in my ideal job are: (e.g., group practice environment — single or multi-specialty; hospital administration; work outside group practice)

The things **I DON'T WANT TO DO** ever again are: (e.g., work 80 hours per week)

7. Can I actively discuss five of my most satisfying accomplishments and achievements in health care?

❏ Yes   ❏ No

In areas outside of health care?

❏ Yes   ❏ No

8. If asked right now, can I clearly and confidently discuss the 10 skills that motivate and energize me?

❏ Yes   ❏ No

I feel my strongest skills are:

The skills I would like to improve are:

9. If I were to use my resume tomorrow, would it highlight my accomplishments and does it incorporate the strengths I stated earlier when I was describing myself?

❏ Yes   ❏ No

What do I need to do now to update my resume?

Do I know how to customize my resume to the unique needs of those I send it to?

10. Who are the first 20 people I would contact as network resources?

11. Can I write a cover letter (to accompany my resume) that quickly gets a reader's attention by linking my skills and accomplishments with that reader's needs?
❑ Yes ❑ No

What do I need to do to prepare myself?

12. If I scheduled a job interview tomorrow, do I have the competence to plan for and succeed in it?
❑ Yes ❑ No

What do I need to do to prepare myself?

13. Do I have written, specific, achievable career goals and objectives?
❑ Yes ❑ No

14. Do I have a self-marketing plan complete with goals, action steps and timetable?
❑ Yes ❑ No

NOTES

If so, does it include:

- An assessment of my skills, interests, values and preferences?
  ❑ Yes   ❑ No

- A written statement of my personal vision and mission?
  ❑ Yes   ❑ No

- Career goals and objectives?
  ❑ Yes   ❑ No

- An updated resume?
  ❑ Yes   ❑ No

- Assessments of environmental and cultural factors, such as industry and market outlook, family interests, location preferences, etc.?
  ❑ Yes   ❑ No

- Research and evaluation opportunities?
  ❑ Yes   ❑ No

- Ways to develop skills in interviewing, networking, negotiating and self-expression?
  ❑ Yes   ❑ No

- Financial-planning information?
  ❑ Yes   ❑ No

15. Have I selected a support person(s) to join me in my quest?
❑ Yes   ❑ No

16. Is now the time to explore how career planning might help me?
❑ Yes   ❑ No

Now that you've thought about these questions, you may have reached one of two conclusions:

1. "Wow, I really need to control my career. I feel I'm not in control now. If the worst should happen — I lose my job — I would NOT be able to start a job search quickly. In fact, I'm not even certain I would want to stay in group or hospital administration."

    or

2. "I'm doing as much as I can at this point. I believe I'm controlling my career as well as I can. I feel confident that I could start a job search quickly because I do know what I want in a next job or career. I am up to date with all the information and material I need to begin a job search."

Summarize your thoughts and reactions. If you're closer to the first response, take time now to brainstorm key action items you will hold yourself accountable for over the next few months. Then, read on to learn more about long-range planning. If you're closer to the second, check your perceptions against my recommendations in this book to help refine your job-search tools. Either way, I have much more to share with you.

Develop a long-term plan and objectives for your career

If you've been thinking about your career but don't know how to get started, here's what you need to do. Start by assessing yourself — identifying your "career self." Through self-assessment, you'll be able to answer the key question "who am I?" by accurately describing your key personal values, interests, skills, satisfying achievements and environment. In addition, you'll have used this information about yourself to develop a personal mission statement. In *How to Find the Work You Love,* Laurence G. Boldt

19

NOTES

says your natural vocation or calling — your life's work — is your unique and living answer to the question, "What am I here to do on this earth?" Boldt reminds us:

> "As individuals, we each comprise a unique constellation of talents, abilities and innate interests. Working in a way that takes advantage of our unique talents, abilities and interests means working with our strengths. Many people spend their whole lives working against their strengths — doing work not really suited to their abilities. The key is to find the work you were born to do — the one thing that takes full advantage of your special talents, interests and abilities. This brings not only greater effectiveness but greater joy." [2]

This joy is what you'll discover in career satisfaction — when your work, leisure and personal time are in balance. Just as your organization may have a mission statement, you should have one you're committed to meeting through your work.

For example, in 1986 I had been employed in the same job for six years and was beginning to ask myself, "What do I want to do when I grow up?" In other words, how do I want to spend the next 5 - 7 years? I decided to go through career planning. As I explored my values, interests, preferences, skills and working environments, I was able to develop the following mission statement:

> "I value the opportunity to consult and counsel with individuals and groups on career-development issues, so they learn how to gather and use information that enhances their personal and professional lives."

[2]How to find the work you love, Laurence G. Boldt; Penguin Books; 1996.

Here are two that administrators of medical groups developed:

> "Create effective solutions to felt needs of people or organizations, so they feel worthy from what was created and put these solutions into action for themselves (with my help)."

and,

> "Create a better world by helping people and organizations define their purpose, reach for meaningful and important goals, achieve alignment with their goals, and achieve balance in their lives. To help others see the whole as well as the parts. Teach others how to become learners for life, and to see the possibilities."

Once you know your career self and your mission, you can begin to define career options and goals, including the type of work and organization that best match your needs and mission.

This is important information to have about yourself. You are now able to confidently evaluate options and opportunities presented to you or those you discover. You don't have to accept a job that a merger or integration may have created, based only on your feeling that it "sounds interesting and may provide a welcome change from what I'm doing now" or "that you are "relieved to be offered ANY job!" You can expertly analyze the new opportunity in terms of the information learned from your self-assessment. Your decision becomes one based on data and facts, not emotion — a powerful outcome.

To reinforce these ideas about career planning, consider this success story. I had a client who worked for a medical center that was merging with another. As Director of Business Services, she was one of two people being considered for a new position — Director of Financial Services for the new, larger, integrated organization. The financial manager of the other organization was

NOTES

the second candidate. This opportunity meant a promotion, raise and greater responsibility — a logical career step for my client.

Why then, was she uncomfortable and having mixed feelings about even applying? Through self-assessment, she discovered:

- She is motivated by challenging projects and solving tough problems;

- She likes to identify problems, develop her own game plan, and then work without too many "guidelines" and "interference" from management policies and procedures; and

- She doesn't find "managing" very motivating. To manage is to be responsible for many bureaucratic policies and procedures required in large health care organizations. She also recognized that supervising people and having to deal with their day-to-day issues weren't her "cup of tea."

Her discoveries were vital to a rational, unemotional decision, assuming she were offered the newly created job. Knowing these very basic characteristics, we discussed what would probably be the major responsibilities of the new job. Guess what? Most of the responsibilities included managing and supervising — tasks that didn't motivate and energize her.

Looking further, she also discovered the job offered little opportunity for working with creative and challenging projects — activities that did energize and motivate her . . . activities she highly valued. She had found the reason for her mixed emotions.

Armed with this information, we reviewed her alternatives. The outcome: She identified a new and temporary position we called Integration Specialist. She sold it as an 18- to 24-month project — a new position through which she would work with both organizations on special merger projects. It met her need for challenge and creativity and the organization's need for a smooth transition. As it turned out, the other person accepted the new director job — managing and supervising met his personal needs. The new, integrated medical center benefited in both situations. Eighteen months after beginning that new project, my client was busy looking for the next new project, or challenge, within the same organization. The moral to this story? Know yourself and have a career plan:

1. Discover your career self;
2. Define your career goals; and
3. Develop a specific, yet flexible career plan.

Through this effort and commitment, you can take control of your career. You can make quality decisions for yourself.

Chapter 3

Take charge of marketing yourself

How can I succeed in my job search?

In this chapter, we'll explore strategies you can use immediately to position yourself for a successful job search. We'll review the important elements of your self-marketing portfolio. To be successful in your job search, you must:

1. Define your career goal(s) so you can articulate reasons for (or against) applying for a specific job. Clearly defined career goals also affect how you come across in cover letters, resumes and interviews.

   In presentations to more than 2,500 medical-group administrators, managers, nurses and physicians, I've found fewer than 25 – only one percent – who said they had a written career plan, including goals. My experience shows this statistic isn't unique to health care. It holds up in high-tech fields as well as in manufacturing, telecommunications, education and government.

2. Recognize you're selling a commodity – YOU. Your job is to uncover implicit and explicit needs of the hiring manager or organization and to show how your skills and experience match those needs.

3. Understand what I refer to as the five "Vs" of marketing yourself:

   - Value
   - Vision
   - Visibility
   - Volition
   - Versatility

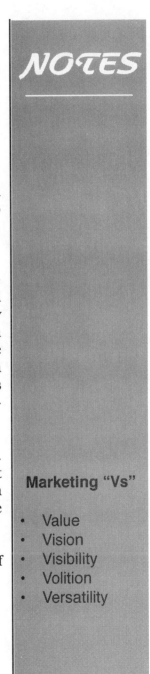

NOTES

Marketing "Vs"

- Value
- Vision
- Visibility
- Volition
- Versatility

4. Select from the various search strategies, including want ads, search and placement firms, networking, marketing or proposal letters, and the Internet.

5. Create a personal or resume database as the first step in marketing yourself.

To move through these five steps, you need a self-marketing plan that includes these key elements:

1. Where do I begin? Plan before you act;

2. Understand yourself – your strengths and how they translate to career self-reliance and career satisfaction;

3. Have clearly defined career goals and plans;

4. Know what you're selling and marketing and to whom you're selling and marketing it;

5. Develop your self-marketing plan – strategies that meet your goals;

6. Understand your audience – how they make decisions, what their needs are; and

7. Develop your personal selling and marketing tools – organize your material to address the needs of hiring managers and organizations.

Where do I begin? Develop your career plan

Of the people I talk to, 98 percent instinctively feel that a job search involves three steps: first, "put together my resume;" second, "locate and talk with one or two head hunters": and third, "send my resume to as many people I can think of." Often, they say something like: "I know my effort will result in several offers from which I can choose the one that best interests me. I know this works because it's always worked in the past." As my clients have found, it doesn't work. Times have changed!

26

Instead, you must do several things BEFORE you even think about preparing a resume, talking with a search firm, or talking with someone from your network. To take charge of your job search and most effectively use time and effort, try a very different approach. You must base your job-search related decisions on knowledge about yourself, your career goals and your plans. So making decisions about your job search – taking charge of it – begins with developing a personal career plan. To meet your ultimate goal (career satisfaction) and to make positive career-related decisions in the future, do what one one percent of health professionals do: take time to think about and develop your road map, your career plan.

Career planning is a systematic way of determining your values, interests, skills, likes, dislikes and preferred cultural work environment. You can evaluate options or alternatives against this information, establish specific goals, and develop plans for achieving your goals. Career planning also means thinking strategically – looking ahead and making some "best guesses" about what the organization will need next year and the year after that. Then, develop your skills so you remain employable to your organization two years down the road.

Mergers and affiliations of medical groups and hospitals are wreaking havoc with the health care environment. Those of you who joined a small group of physicians probably did so for a reason – you like working directly with patients and the physicians. Maybe you like "calling the shots" or being "in charge." Suddenly, along comes a merger with several other medical groups or an integration with a large hospital. The environment has changed, in some instances overnight. The new organization may create a culture that isn't consistent with your values or a working environment you can't embrace. The change in the environment creates severe career "dis-ease" for you. Knowing what kind of environment energizes and motivates you is critical to your job search.

NOTES

Understanding yourself – your strengths. Answer three questions:

Who am I?

Self-discovery is a powerful job-search tool. Answering this question involves investigating and identifying your personal values, interests, likes, dislikes and skills that energize and motivate. Self-discovery helps you to identify important preferences, culture, work environment, and the type of colleagues you want to work with. The result: A database of information that you can use to evaluate and analyze future career or job options and opportunities.

Where am I going?

This question relates to your career plan, or the direction you want to take in your career. It's looking at the information uncovered during self-discovery and making some educated decisions about your future direction.

Initially you may identify several career plans or, at least, several options. You may bring into focus a practical career goal that is reachable within your current organization or profession. You only have to negotiate the change. You also may identify an ideal career goal or job – perhaps more than one. They may not be practical and "doable" now, but with a little planning, creativity, and maybe professional development, they could be. You may need to identify and carry out a practical, short-term plan that helps you reach this long-term goal – this "dream." I've worked with clients whose dreams have come true. Think about it – this could be you!

Here's an example of how self-assessment and developing a plan helped one client – his dream did come true. Through his self-assessment, a client with a CPA certificate and more than 10 years of accounting and audit experience in a

28

large hospital recognized that his true career interest and passion was to be a chef! He remembered that the happiest he had ever been in his work was during undergraduate and graduate school, when he cooked in the school's cafeteria and local restaurants. But he had gone into accounting because his father was a CPA and "strongly encouraged" him to take the same track. Just before our fourth career-planning session, he told me he had decided to enroll in a culinary school for the upcoming fall. Over the summer, he was going to Las Vegas and get a job in a "fine" restaurant. When asked about how he felt his dad would react, he responded "I've spent the past 10 years doing what my dad thought was the job I should have. I now realize how unhappy I really was. Finally, I've made a decision for myself."

In this example my client decided that the appropriate short-term goal was to find temporary work in a related job – for the experience – before beginning his culinary education. You may not be as adventurous, or you may have family commitments. If so, and it's impractical for you to abruptly pull up stakes and relocate, try an alternative. For example, maybe you can develop the necessary skills or get the relevant degree while remaining in your job. So your choices might be to:

- Make no changes in your status. Set a financial goal to achieve before "making the move";

- Take evening or weekend classes, get the degree, then market yourself into a different profession;

- Negotiate changes in your job to get a closer match to your personal profile while still taking evening or weekend classes; or

- Work part-time and enroll in school full-time.

Each of these alternatives will head you in the right direction. Some will get you there quicker than others. You can probably think of other alternatives that fit your situation – limited only by your personal circumstances and creativity.

Action Steps

• Research
   opportunities.

• Negotiate
   changes.

• Create develop-
   ment plan.

• Volunteer.

• Market yourself.

How do I get to where I want to go?

Answering this question leads you into action – taking that important first step to change your career and life forever, rather than waiting and waiting but never making a decision.

A few years ago, I presented a workshop on "Career Planning – Positioning Yourself for Your Future" at an annual Anesthesia Administration Assembly. It happened to be in San Francisco. Having dinner one evening at one of those outdoor winery restaurants that you can find only in Northern California, I happened to overhear a conversation about jobs between a couple behind me. At one point in the conversation I heard one person say, "I guess I can put up with my job. After all, I have only 10 years until retirement." Now, stop and think for a minute about this statement. Have you, at some point in your career, said this to yourself? Here was a person who was clearly dissatisfied with his job and the company he worked. Rather than act, his choice seemed to be to do nothing, to put up with his dissatisfaction and exist until retirement. There's a better alternative – you can do something. All you have to do is decide to act by:

• Researching opportunities;
• Negotiating a change with your current employer;
• Creating a personal plan for professional development;
• Volunteering in school, hospitals or community programs; or
• Marketing yourself to another organization.

Research opportunities.

Research those different career goals you identified earlier. You might decide to do information interviews with people in similar jobs or companies – gathering as much data as you can so you can analyze it against the information you uncovered during self-discovery. In this way, you can align your values, interests and skills that energize and motivate you with the culture, work environment, and colleagues you will work with best.

Research helps you narrow your potential options and decide which to pursue first – your practical goal or your ideal goal. Let me explain. A practical goal may be similar to your current work but better match your self-assessment. It may be more "practical" in the short term. Once you're working in that area, you can lay the foundation for accomplishing your ideal goal. You may go back to school to get a degree in that field or save enough money to move to an ideal job in the future. In this case, the practical job becomes the means to an end.

Here's what one client decided to do. This client dreamed of starting up her own, home-based, consulting business. However, it wasn't practical in her case to abruptly resign her job as a medical practice administrator and open a consulting business. As a single mother, she couldn't walk away from a consistent income and risk opening a new small business. She had two children close to high-school graduation and college bills to come.

This client set a goal. Her goal statement: "In five years I will be working for myself as a health care consultant." With this goal, she began planning and doing things that moved her toward that goal. Her action plan included:

- Budgeting over the next five years, including college expenses and savings to cover expenses once she begins the consulting practice. Her financial goal was to have 12 months of income in savings;

- Researching how to set up a small consulting business, including writing a business plan, marketing, initial capital, developing a client base, etc.;

NOTES

- Researching current and future trends in health care, specifically the future trends for the area in which she planned to consult; and

- Developing skills in specific areas and technologies. She wanted to take classes in promoting and marketing a small consulting practice.

Included in her plan was to find two or three small consulting projects she could do, on her own time, while employed. She wanted to expand her experience and credibility before going out on her own. She identified projects relating to her job that added to her experience.

The conclusion to this story is yet to be written. We won't know if she reaches her goal for another four years. But, she is committed to meeting her five-year goal. As a result, she and her medical group receive two immediate benefits: (1) she's motivated and energized about her work, so work is actually "fun" again; and (2) in her quest to find related projects that increase her experience, she has uncovered several that will benefit the group.

Yes, this can happen to you. But, it won't come looking for you. You must create the opportunity yourself. Your dream can come true – if you work for it. Go for it! Make it happen!

Negotiate a change with your current employer.

Explore all options within your medical group. If you negotiate a change in your current job or work environment, it may allow you to move to an area or into responsibilities that more closely match your personal preferences and profile. But you must propose the changes.

Many times clients discover better-matching jobs within their own organizations. For example, a colleague and I have done one-to-one sessions for career consulting with more than 500 managers and engineers within a Fortune 500 computer hardware manufacturer. Fewer than one percent have left the company. In most instances, managers have found jobs within the company (some in other locations) that better fit their personal profile. In some cases, they simply needed to negotiate a change with their manager – taking on new but energizing assignments while dropping the more boring and mundane tasks. Projects you eliminate or download will find their match in people who see them as challenging. Everyone finds opportunities; everyone wins.

Create a personal plan for professional development.

The data you uncover from information interviews may help you decide that additional education would better position you for future advancement within your organization or would make you more marketable to other organizations. Depending on your goals, you might decide to "get that graduate degree" or "finally complete that undergraduate degree I started a few years ago." You could decide to enroll in a certificate program offered by many professional associations. For example, the Medical Group Management Association (MGMA) offers certification through the American College of Medical Practice Executives (ACMPE). After meeting all graduation requirements, you become a Fellow. The Healthcare Financial Management Association (HFMA) has two professional certifications. One is the Certified Healthcare Financial Professional and the other is the Fellow. The requirements for each of these certifications easily mirror the curriculum for a graduate degree and are very well respected within the profession.

Here's an example. A recent client, an administrator at an independent, four-physician practice, identified a career goal – become the chief financial officer of a medium-sized hospital. From information interviews, he recognized he lacked the required graduate degree.

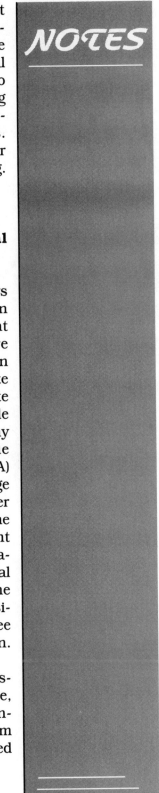

NOTES

My client decided to enroll in a weekend program for executives seeking the Master's Degree in Business Administration – specializing in finance and accounting. After the first year of graduate school, he decided to enroll in the Healthcare Financial Management Association's program to become a Certified Healthcare Financial Professional. His goal: within three years, have the education and professional experience necessary to become the chief financial officer in a hospital.

Volunteer.

Your volunteer activities should satisfy some part of your career goal. You may decide to volunteer in your child's school district as a parent counselor or part-time teacher's aide. You may decide to sit on the school board because you are concerned about the quality of education for children. Or, you may volunteer in your church or other agency in your home town.

One of my clients had a very strong value of preserving the beauty and green space in the community where he lives. He was very concerned about how a non-stop, uncontrolled building boom was quickly taking over greenbelt areas around town. He decided to commit personal time to work with several citizen groups who help the city council develop better ways to monitor building permits and subdivision plans. They established two goals: develop a master plan and ensure all new housing developments conform to it; and get the city to buy greenbelt areas and set aside land for parks and for bicycles and hiking paths.

Market yourself to another organization.

You may decide to find another job outside your organization. Once you've made this decision, your job is to develop a plan that answers key questions. What kind of job should I look for? What environment is the best match to my values,

34

interests, skills, etc. Do I want to stay in health care? What other industries "fit" my needs?

Here's an example. The medical group where a client had been an administrator for more than eight years recently affiliated with an integrated hospital system. The working environment changed dramatically. His job changed. Soon, he was feeling real stress and uncertainty about his job. The bottom line – he didn't like how his job changed, but didn't know what he should do.

After completing his career plan, he recognized his best work would be managing a group practice with five - ten physicians in a single specialty where he was directly involved in all decisions that affected the group. He also recognized he liked occasional contact with patients. Evaluating his "ideal" setting against the environment created by the integration, he quickly recognized why he was feeling so much "dis-ease." He decided to search for a smaller group practice; one that didn't intend to affiliate with a larger hospital system.

This situation is typical. Most administrators wait until the integration or merger has taken place BEFORE acting and then "hope" they'll match with the new environment. Or privately a person may say "I have only 10 years until early retirement; I'll stick it out." The result of this type of decision is probably 10 years of "existing" while productivity and motivation decrease. Someone like this may not make it to retirement; the organization may decide to change managers, especially if his or her productivity declines.

Why wait? Decide before the integration. Take control of the decisions that affect your career.

Know what you are selling

In a single word – you are selling "YOU!" I've found that it's useful to think of five Vs when marketing yourself: value, volition, versatility, visibility, and vision.

Show your value

Value means demonstrating your "worth" to the organization. You must: 1) Discuss your background, achievements and accomplishments in terms of bottom-line results to the organization and the hiring manager; 2) Discuss your previous experience in terms the hiring manager will understand and connect with emotionally; 3) Get the hiring manager to say, "If I hire you, here's how you'll help me achieve my goals and objectives; here's what you'll contribute to the bottom line of my department; and 4) Think in terms of future contributions you can make to the organization – how your experiences, accomplishments and achievements will help them meet their strategic goals. Your ability to communicate value is critical to your success.

Have volition

Volition refers to a willingness to make decisions, to help the organization meet its goals and objectives. It's how you show energy, creativity, enthusiasm and motivation when talking to a prospective hiring manager or contact. One way to demonstrate volition is how you describe previous accomplishments. Another is exhibiting a determination to succeed as well as showing flexibility and adaptability to change. After you finish an interview, you want the hiring manager or contact to think, "That's a person with a lot of energy and who is not afraid to make decisions. I sense a lot of commitment and motivation. I know this person would bring a lot to our group."

Show your versatility

Versatility refers to your flexibility and adaptability. It's your ability to change easily and "willingly" from one task to another, to take on different projects, or to work with different groups and people. It means you're comfortable thinking "outside the box" – not getting caught up in the "we've always done it this way" attitude and refusing to embrace change.

The key to revealing your flexibility and adaptability is how you describe past accomplishments in terms of different approaches to problem solving, looking for unique solutions, or showing you're not intimidated by the unknown. Versatility, flexibility and adaptability may be the three most critical traits organizations now require of their managers.

Create visibility

Visibility means creating or identifying opportunities for yourself. It's what allows you to maintain a high profile within your profession. Visibility refers to involvement – how involved are you within your profession and specialty area? In other words – are you known around town? Are you using your network contacts wisely and effectively? Are your contacts and resources looking for opportunities to refer to you?

Have vision

Vision also refers to mission. Have you learned enough about yourself to know and understand what type of work truly energizes and motivates you? What are the work activities and surroundings that allow you to "jump out of bed before the alarm goes off" because you're so excited about your work and what you're doing that you can't wait to get going?

In addition, are you able to:

• Visualize outcomes and results of marketing yourself;

• Describe your past accomplishments and achievements so they relate to an identified future vision or goal;

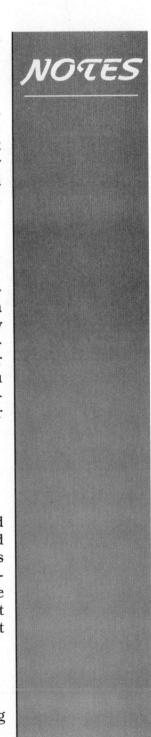

- Define the future for yourself and the organization; and

- Demonstrate unusual and creative ideas or perceptions, imagine new products or services, foresee ways to restructure and plan.

Develop your resume database

I'd like to introduce you to a concept I've used successfully with hundreds of clients. Think about this question: What's the purpose of marketing yourself? This answer is easy. It's to get a job in a field or organization that is ideally matched to your career goals, leading to career satisfaction. Then, what's the only purpose of your resume? No, it's not to get you that ideal job. It's to get a face-to-face discussion or interview. This could be a self-marketing discussion in which you describe your background and experience to someone. Or, it could be a job interview. In other words, through your resume (and cover letter), your objective is to persuade the reader to pick up the phone and schedule an interview. After that, it's up to you to sell yourself.

Here's another question. Why would someone who doesn't know you want to schedule a discussion or interview? What is it about your resume that would motivate a stranger to call? The answer – somewhere in your resume and cover letter you connected with that reader; somehow, *you matched your background, experiences, accomplishments and skills to the needs and requirements of the reader and organization.*

Look at the situation this way. A hiring organization has to find someone who matches closely with its needs and requirements so problems get solved and decisions get made that meet its objectives. The only way you'll persuade the reader to call is if you can show how – because of your background, skills and experience – you can accomplish what the organization needs. And it's all based on what you have put in your resume.

Here's the catch. You must match your skills and experience with these needs in 15 seconds. That's right, 15 seconds. In talking with hundreds of hiring managers, I've learned their initial screening decision occurs in the first 15 seconds of reading. That's not a lot of time to convince a stranger, especially when that person may be reviewing 50 - 100 resumes at once.

I know how the process usually works. When you apply for a certain job, you pull your "one-size-fits-all" resume (which may be type set) out of a folder or print it from your computer. Then you send it off, hoping to get a response. When you use the same resume every time, for every opportunity, you are spinning the wheel of fortune. For those times when you got a favorable response, LUCK was probably on your side. The reader connected with some tidbit of information on your resume – in 15 seconds. Something caught his or her eye.

Don't base your job search success on luck! I'm going to describe a process that will increase your chances of connecting with that reader. I won't go so far as to suggest it's fool proof. But I do have many specific examples in which managers had been searching without any response, not even receiving the famous form letter saying the company received your resume and would keep it on file for six months. Within a few weeks of following this approach, they were getting phone calls, which allowed them to get face-to-face interviews.

To get that all-important phone call, create a personal database

A personal or resume database kept in a file on your computer will help you create attention-getting cover letters and resumes. Think of a resume database as a comprehensive listing of accomplishments from all your jobs, volunteer assignments and personal activities.

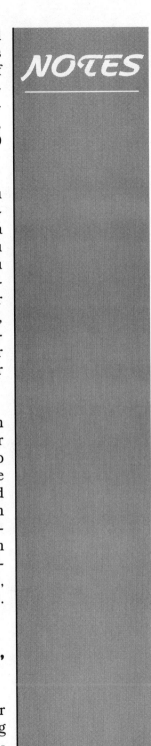

NOTES

Your objective is to write a short, yet descriptive story for each accomplishment, task or project. Each story should be two to three sentences, describing what you did and any outcome or result for each activity. At this point, don't worry about length or wordiness. Brainstorm every aspect of each assignment, project and task. A typical database could be 10 to 25 pages.

It may help to organize your thoughts and work by thinking chronologically. Start with your most recent accomplishment or project, probably one you've just completed, and work backwards. Sounds impossible, but I've found that once you begin, your mind starts working – you recall examples and projects long since forgotten.

How does a resume database help in your job search? Remember, for your job search to succeed, you have to show how your experience and background match the needs of the prospective employer. To demonstrate a match, you must be able to recall quickly any relevant accomplishment or example from your past and describe it in terms of the prospective employer's needs. What makes this difficult is that you never know when you might need to recall an example on the spot.

Preparation is the key. Taking time BEFORE you need to recall the information may eliminate any hesitation or feeling of "I wish I would have remembered that example" as you drive away from an interview or review a cover letter recently sent. Sometimes you may still have that feeling, but the more time you put into recreating your past and thinking about all those long forgotten experiences, the more likely you'll recall pertinent examples as you need them.

Use information sources to complete your database

Information sources are available to help you recall details. For example, locate and review all previous job descriptions. They will provide good clues about your activities during that period. Review written performance evaluations from previous years. They should mention projects or assignments you were involved with. If you didn't keep copies (and you should), check with your boss (current and past), as well as the human resource department.

Talk with colleagues, co-workers, supervisors and peers – current and past. They're a great resource. They may also be able to recall other people you've worked with and long since forgotten. These could be people who also worked on the project or were associated with it in some way.

It's important to include detail for at least the previous 10 years; it's also useful to include data from your entire work and personal life, even if it goes "back" 20 years. You never know when you might be able to use an example from that part of your past to demonstrate your expertise or show how you are proficient in a particular skill.

Don't forget to include activities from your volunteer work with schools, church, United Way and other organizations. Remember, you NEVER know when you will want to use one of your past activities to demonstrate your value to someone. One of my clients included his experience as a Boy Scout leader on his resume. In one instance the interviewer had similar experience. Finding this common ground, my client was able to develop a positive relationship – to create a bond that eventually led to a job offer. The moral of this story – you never know when, or how, some aspect of your history will be useful in connecting with someone. This is why it's so critical to include EVERYTHING from your background on the resume database.

If this project looks too hard, take heart from others

Clients consistently report that, at least initially, they thought it would be difficult or even impossible to re-create their past in this much detail. However, once started they report:

- "Previous job descriptions and my performance reviews were a wealth of information."

- "I had completely forgotten a couple of major projects I had completed just two years ago. In fact, I could have used those as examples in my most recent interview."

- "Forcing myself to think about my past accomplishments turned out to be a very motivating and energizing activity. I hadn't really thought about how successful I had been over the years. It's easy to lose sight of past successes in the face of current problems."

- "Initially, I could not get past the feeling that I really hadn't done anything unique – that I was 'just doing my job' – but once I started thinking about my past work and activity, I recognized I've accomplished a lot and I do have very transferable skills that employers need and are looking for."

This is a common response I get from clients when I ask them to think about their past in terms of "what they have accomplished." We can lose sight of real accomplishments when we are continually bombarded with current problems, crises, new projects, and just the daily crunch of work. It's very energizing and eye opening to re-create your past in terms of real accomplishments. You haven't had any reason to think of your past experience as outcomes or results someone else might be interested in. By describing yourself in terms of outcomes, you demonstrate your value – to others, any maybe more importantly, to yourself.

Get started by thinking about specific results

Get started. Draft your resume database. Don't put it off. It won't get easier if your wait. In fact, you will soon complete the project you're working on at this moment. Make sure it gets on your database too. Can you recall those two projects just recently completed?

Use two key questions to shape your database stories

To craft your database stories, ask yourself two questions:

1) What did I do when I did that? and,
2) So what?

These questions help you expand your thinking about each project. The first question, "What did I do when I did that?" helps define what you actually did when you worked on and completed the project. It also helps you determine what actions you took, such as researching, designing or completing a new process or system. The question "So what?" helps you determine specific outcomes or results. Once you think in terms of outcomes or results, it's easier for you to understand and discuss how the result of that project or task contributed to the organization's bottom line.

Here are three examples of how clients used these questions to write stories for their resume database.

Example 1: In reviewing a client's resume, I found this accomplishment statement:

Involved in the sale of the clinic to the local hospital.

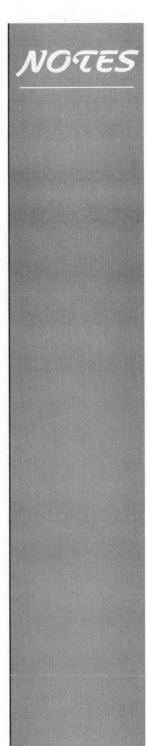

NOTES

43

At first glance, we may think it's a good statement. But let's look at it again. Is it clear? Concise? Yes, it is. However, does it describe what this person did and the result? No, it doesn't. In fact, someone may read this and say to themselves – "So what? I've read other resumes where the person was involved in a clinic sale. What makes this one different? Why should I call this person and not any of the others I've read?"

In our work together, I asked my client *"What did you do when you were involved in the sale of the clinic to the local hospital?"* Here's how she expanded on her original statement:

I provided leadership role in the sale of the clinic to a nonprofit hospital, giving physicians all the pertinent information and data about the sale including:

- *Collected and analyzed all financial information concerning the sale and discussed implications and ramifications with physicians;*

- *Researched all equity issues related to the sale including asset distribution to owners, potential of collecting outstanding receivables, and appraised all equipment;*

- *Conducted a good-will analysis of the ambulatory surgery center; and*

- *Helped evaluate corporate cultures of all entities; devised two programs to help successfully assimilate cultures.*

And this list could be expanded. On the surface, we tend to think in terms of helping with the sale of the clinic, but it's really much more than that. It's thinking in terms of those critical activities that made the sale of the clinic a **success.** These are the skills, the behaviors, that help make you stand out; that demonstrate your uniqueness and value to someone reading your resume or interviewing you. It's this "expanded" statement, including bullet points, that is included in your resume database.

44

Example 2: A client's accomplishment statement read:

Administered and maintained physician employment agreements.

It's a good statement, but the reader could say, "So what? Nearly every administrator applying for this position has dealt with physician employment agreements."

How could this applicant expand on the statement to describe better what he did when he administered and maintained physician employment agreements. Here's what my client came up with after thinking about the questions, *"What did I do when I did that?"* and *"So what?"*

Administered and maintained physician employment agreements:

- *Did financial analysis to ensure physicians' salaries met minimum production goals;*

- *Renegotiated all physician contracts as they came due;*

- *Did financial analysis to determine physician-bonus amounts; explained process and results to physicians; responded to questions and concerns; and*

- *Advised physicians on the benefits available under their contracts.*

Example 3: Here's another accomplishment statement. It does answer the question "So what?" by indicating a result:

Managed a small ambulatory surgery center increasing use by 45 percent over three years.

It can still be improved. The expanded version is:

Managed a small ambulatory surgery center increasing use by 45 percent over three-year period:

45

- *Researched new and expanded services offered through the surgery center including surveying needs of customers and patients, break-even financial analysis, and availability of resources to provide services. The result: three new specialty procedures were added to the clinic's services and the center did more than two times the planned procedures in the first year;*

- *Increased use by bringing ophthalmologists from the community into the clinic to do cataract surgery. Showed patients they could save money compared to undergoing the same procedures as hospital outpatients;*

- *Did all analysis to determine actual fixed, variable, direct and indirect center costs. Data allowed board to make informed decisions as to what procedures to continue and whether to purchase vs. lease specialized equipment;*

- *Credentialed new and existing medical staff on an on-going basis;*

- *Successfully managed all state health department inspections and national certifications; and*

- *Increased the use of center by exploring and signing an rental agreement with an optomologist from a neighboring community to see patients referred by center physicians.*

Length is not a concern for your resume database. Remember, this is your database; it's not the document you would give someone. You'll create a short version for each opportunity – customized to specific needs.

Maintain your resume database

Consider your resume database as a work in progress, always adding information. Don't be surprised if you continue to recall projects or assignments previously forgotten. Some clients report waking during the night because they suddenly remember a past assignment. One client was attending the symphony when an idea surfaced. Be ready to write a note, wherever you are. Add it to your database. Computers and word- processing make it easy to update and modify.

Always make one, even two backup files of your database. You don't want to re-create it from scratch!

Get busy – create your resume database. Don't procrastinate!

Use your database while considering your job-search alternatives

OKAY, now what? You've labored, struggled and fumed over re-creating and documenting your past; you've made two backup copies.

First, congratulate yourself. You've created a living and valuable document that has many critical uses in your job search. In addition to providing the basis for each customized resume, the database will help you to:

1) Write effective or proposal letters;
2) Create cover letters and letters of introduction that quickly get a reader's attention;
3) Prepare for and undergo job interviews more confidently and competently;
4) Decide whom to contact for scheduling of information interviews; and
5) Review and identify activities and accomplishments that truly energize and motivate you, and those that don't. Knowing this information will provide clues as to the kind of work and environment to look for in future opportunities.

Job-Search Alternatives

- Networking

- Marketing letters

- Ads

- Search firms

- Cold calls

- Internet

- Luck

Job-search alternatives

It's important to get your job search started correctly. Take time before actually beginning your search to consider available alternatives. Know enough about each to be able to select ones that will give you the greatest return on your investment. In this section, I'll describe seven alternatives in order of importance and payoff:

1. Networking: Identifying and using your personal contacts;
2. Directing marketing letters to selected companies or individuals;
3. Working with executive search firms;
4. Responding to ads in newspapers and professional trade journals;
5. Using the Internet;
6. Making "cold" calls; and
7. Relying on old-fashioned luck.

Here are my thoughts and experiences with each.

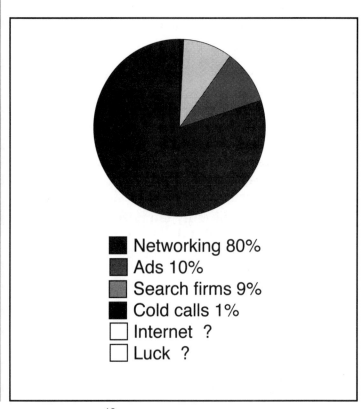

- ■ Networking 80%
- ■ Ads 10%
- ■ Search firms 9%
- ■ Cold calls 1%
- □ Internet ?
- □ Luck ?

Networking: Identifying and using your personal contacts

Much has been written about networking so I'm not going to go into detail here. Instead, I want to highlight the important aspects of networking and discuss why you should consider it the most critical tool in your job-search tool kit.

The word *network* is overused, so commonplace – such a catch-all phrase – that I fear some people feel it has outlived its usefulness. Yet, statistics indicate that about 80 percent of all jobs are found using networking. It's a way to develop qualified contacts, leads and other resources so critical to a successful job search.

The word *network*, when used as a noun, is an informal system of un-associated people linked by shared interests or values. Networks are made up of self-reliant people and independent groups.

When used as a verb, networking means people connecting – contacting and talking – with people. In other words, one person with a need identifies and contacts another person whose position or status makes him or her, a resource. With contact and discussion, networking begins. Think of your networking list as your contact list.

Despite some contrary opinions, networking is not a way to find a job. Networking is a process of connecting with someone to exchange information or collect information. It's a key element in researching potential markets and for marketing yourself. You can't do information interviews without using people from your network. It's your opportunity to find out as much as you can about a preferred industry or organization before you formally apply.

Purpose of networking in job search.

Networking in job search has two main purposes: to research the job market and to uncover job leads from the hidden job market.

NOTES

NOTES

As a strategic tool for market research, networking is a way to:

- Define and develop an understanding of your particular job market and the needs and requirements of that market;

- Uncover the names of companies, or people within companies, who may need someone with your experience and background;

- Identify current and future trends or needs and patterns within an industry or organization; and

- Determine which organizations are the best personal fit for you and the best people to contact in those organizations.

As a method of finding job leads from the hidden job market, networking helps you access those hidden job leads. Given the notion that about 60 percent of all jobs are not published in any form, it's your job to tap this rich source of potential jobs – to uncover job leads. Employers typically use their own established informal networks to locate job candidates rather than classified ads, so you must connect with people who know – or know someone who knows – about leads.

To be effective at networking, you must:

1. *Have a clear career goal or objective.*

You must be reasonably sure of where you want to go next in your career, the skills that motivate and energize you, and the general nature of the work you are looking for – your career goal. You cannot appear undecided or non-committal with people in your network. You may have two or even three ideas – areas you want to research or explore. But you can't come across as "wishy-washy."

2. *Have a succinct self-presentation.*

I call this a 2-1/2 minute drill. (Please refer to Chapter 6 on interviewing for a detailed discussion of this technique.) It's a brief presentation which describes who you are, your background experiences, and what you are looking for – all in about two minutes.

3. *Do market research.*

You must complete detailed research in the market areas which interest you including organizations within those market areas. For example, suppose you want to transition into a large regional hospital in a metropolitan area, but you work in a rural regional medical center. You must research the needs and issues of the large metropolitan hospitals in the location you want to move to; get an idea of future trends and needs; and discover the competencies and skills they are looking for in new hires for that type of work.

4. *Develop your networking list – that extensive list of contacts.*

Brainstorm a list of possible people you can contact. I recommend that clients set a goal of about 300 names. Remember the rules for brainstorming – don't evaluate or judge the quality of the names on your list.

In developing your contact list, consider people:
*   You have access to, who are willing to talk with you;
*   Who are knowledgeable in the areas you are interested in pursuing; and
*   People who know other people – who are good networkers themselves.

Once you start listing names, you will begin to recall people long since forgotten. Think in terms of vendors you've worked with, committees or task forces you've been a part of, etc. Include all activities away from work, including volunteer and personal activities. Don't forget your doctor,

NOTES

dentist, school teachers, etc. I had one client who "found" a valuable network contact by talking with his lawn service. Don't forget the membership directory from either the Medical Group Management Association or the Healthcare Financial Management Association.

Once you've developed your contact list, prioritize in categories like hot, warm, cold or hottest, hot, somewhat warm, warm, cool, and cold. Of course, focus your time on the hot or hottest contacts. They will have the greatest payoff.

Reluctant to network?

You may resist networking, usually because of four common concerns:

1. *Unwillingness to tell others you're looking for a job.*

It's one hurdle you have to overcome – you must become comfortable talking with friends and colleagues about looking for a job. I've found this to be especially true for men. Generally, my male clients seem to resist asking for help. There's the feeling that "I have to solve this problem by myself; I don't need help." Another common statement I hear is "I can do this myself. I don't need help." Here's another interesting observation – once a male becomes comfortable networking, it's usually hard to get him to quit. I've had several male clients who ended up networking "just for the fun of it." I've actually had to curtail their networking activities and get them to focus on the information collected – to move on.

2. *You may be embarrassed to ask for help; your ego gets in the way because it feels like begging.*

It may feel as though you're asking for a favor when you tell others you're networking and the reasons for it. Remember one fact – people want to help and will go out of their way if they feel they can be helpful to you and your job search. In most cases, they won't feel like you are asking for a favor.

3. *It's a new experience for you.*

Networking is a skill everyone must learn. Because it's a new experience you may not feel comfortable using that skill until you've had practice. It will feel clumsy at first. That's okay. It take practice and rehearsal.

I suggest you draft out what you want to say when you contact a network person. Then practice your "networking speech" with a family member or close friend. Ask them for feedback. Networking is a skill. For a new skill to become a habit, you must practice it about 21 times. Practice is vital for networking to become comfortable.

4. *Don't want to hurt a personal relationship.*

This is a sensible concern because you can damage a relationship if you handle networking incorrectly. Never put your network resource on the spot by assuming the person has a job available or knows someone who has an opening. Use those with whom you have a good relationship as a resource for names or contacts you do not know.

Here's what you can do to network successfully.

1. Tell your contact you're looking for a job (in a specific field, organization or position). Be up front and tell the person exactly why you're looking for a job. Don't beat around the bush. Be honest!

2. State why that contact person is in a position to help. The contact may be working in the same type of organization (e.g., multi-specialty group on the East Coast) or have the same type of job you are looking for (group practice administrator).

3. Briefly describe your skills, accomplishments and background. Write a brief script that's a description of your own experiences and skills – as they apply to the job and the person you're talking to.

4. State how you think this person can help. It's critical that you think through and be very clear with them about what you would like them to do and why. Be sure to ask the contact person about others whom you could contact. Expand your contact list.

Use the next four pages to begin your contact list. Keep it with you at all times; continue to add names; brainstorm, don't evaluate.

1.

2.

3.

4.

5.

6.

7.

8.

9.

10.

11.

12.

13.

14.

15.

16.

17.

18.

19.

20.

21.

NOTES

22.

23.

24.

25.

26.

27.

28.

29.

30.

31.

32.

33.

34.

35.

36.

37.

38.

39.

40.

41.

42.

43.

44.

45.

46.

47.

48.

49.

50.

51.

52.

53.

54.

55.

56.

57.
58.

59.

60.

61.

62.

63.

64.

65.

66.

67.

68.

NOTES

69.

70.

71.

72.

73.

74.

75.

76.

77.

78.

79.

80.

81.

82.

83.

84.

85.

86.

87.

88.

89.

90.

Marketing letters to selected companies or individuals

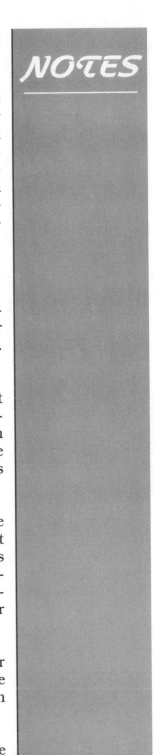

Sometimes referred to as proposal letters, this approach allows you to target specific people or organizations, introduce yourself to them, and tell them when you'll follow up. The typical marketing letter is an expanded cover letter that emphasizes your interests, along with related skills and accomplishments, in exploring possible employment with their organization or in their profession.

Here's how you can use marketing letters:

1. Define the market or industry you are interested in. Conduct research that defines your job market and target specific organizations. Create an initial list of target companies.

2. Research companies and issues. You must do specific research to understand the industry's and target company's issues. Based on this information, you can refine and prioritize your target list – to match the career goals you've set for yourself.

3. Network to get information. This is where your marketing letters are useful. You must identify people to write and talk to; learn as much as you can about the situation or environment so you can customize your marketing material in a way that connects with their interests.

4. Propose yourself as a solution by linking your background and accomplishment with the organization's needs; propose how you can help solve their problems.

The marketing letter helps you identify for the organization or group practice how you can help them solve problems, fill needs, or improve how they work by employing your services in a newly created or existing position. When you have

NOTES

reached this stage, you have something to say which is more credible and memorable than "Please hire me, I want to work with your organization." Instead you're saying, "Here's why you should consider hiring me."

Marketing letters work. Try one!

Working with executive search firms

The common perception among clients is that contacting a "head hunter" is the first step of their job-search process. This is not the case. Here's why. When initially contacted, a search firm may seem excited about working with you. And based on your experience described in your resume, they may give you the impression they have "multiple" opportunities for which you're a good "fit." After the first conversation, you typically don't hear from them again unless they can match your background with a client. In fact, any calls to the representative may go unanswered.

Search firms are paid by the organizations who hire them to fill a position; they work for that organization, not for you. So, don't expect any person from a search firm to be overly responsive to you and your needs past the first phone conversation.

The theme throughout this book is control – what you can do to take as much control of your job search as possible. Working with a recruiter places planning and decisions in the hands of that person. You don't control who recruiters talk to or which organizations they may present you to. They may decide not to present your name to a particular client's organization, and that organization could be high on your list, if you knew about it.

A successful job search depends on building and nurturing your network and developing relationships with people in that network. It's tough to build a relationship with recruiters because their efforts aren't focused on your success.

National statistics suggest you have at most a 9-percent chance of finding a job by using a search firm. So, I advise spending no more than 9 percent of your job-search efforts contacting and working with search firms. Obviously, it has a payoff, it's just a low one.

Contingent and retained search firms

It is important to understand that there are two types of search firms, each with a different focus. There are contingent and retained search firms.

Contingent search firms:

- Are usually used by organizations to locate mid-level and below executives, managers and supervisors at the middle level and below. These are typically positions paying less than $70,000 per year;

- Receive payment ONLY when their candidate is hired;

- Seldom work on an exclusive basis with a hiring organization. They compete with other contingent firms who may know about an open position and also submit candidate names for that position. Contingent recruiters tend to work faster and submit as many candidate names as possible. This means you may be one of many presented to the hiring organization; and

- Will provide you with more exposure than retained firms because they send resumes to many clients. This exposure may be useful in the early stages of your job search. The downside – your resume may be sent to organizations low on your priority list.

Retained search firms:

- Are kept on retainer by a client organization to fill positions as they are needed; they will be asked to find a qualified candidate each time a position opens up;

- Are paid by charging their client organization a fee for every candidate hired;

- Typically are hired to find candidates in positions with salaries of $75,000 per year and higher; and

- Usually present a short list of two or three candidates to the organization. This means the retained firm does all the initial screening of how a candidate matches the position's qualifications and their best guess as to how the candidate will "fit" the organization.

The good news is that if a retained search firm considers you for a specific position, you will be part of a very small group that "made the cut." Notice the issue of control in this situation. Who is making the initial decisions? Of course, it's the search firm that decides YOU are a likely candidate to present to the organization. So, control rests with the search firm, not with you – as it would if you had been able to network into that organization. Controlling as many of the decisions made during your job search is all about building relationships. Placing a lot of importance in a search firm is a very big roadblock in that process. Your goal should be to develop a relationship with a hiring organization, not with a search firm.

With a retained search firm, it's unlikely you'll be "presented" to more than one or two organizations a year. While one recruiter at a firm is using your file, no other recruiter from that same firm can contact you for another assignment, even if you're perceived to be a good match.

If you were hired by an organization through a retained search firm during the past year (in some cases, two years), you are "not available" for positions with other companies, even if you are well qualified. For this reason alone, you must make sure several retained search firms have your resume.

Questions clients often ask about using search firms.

1. *How do I tell if a recruiter is with a contingent or retained search firm?*

When a recruiter contacts you, always ASK if they represent a contingent or retained search firm. Also, ask for detailed background into the assignment before giving your approval to use your resume.

2. *What do I ask first when a search firm contacts me or I contact them?*

Have five or six interview questions ready to ask during the initial phone call. For example:

- Are you a retained or contingent firm?
- How you work with client organizations? With candidates?
- Do you specialize in health care?
- What percentage of your work is in health care?
- For what other industries or professions do you also conduct searches?
- Describe the types of positions you have filled over the past 6 - 12 months.
- Who are your client organizations? (if a retained search firm)
- What types of health care organizations have you successfully placed candidates into during the past 6 - 12 months? (if a contingent search firm)
- Do you focus locally? Regionally? Nationally? Internationally?

What are other questions you might want to ask recruiters when they call? When you contact them? Write them down now.

3. *Should I contact only search firms that specialize in health care positions?*

You should consider using search firms that specialize in health care. They will have developed an extensive and varied list of client organizations. However, don't ignore a general search firm, especially for those higher executive positions. The larger multiple-office search firms will cover all industries but may have specialists in certain areas of expertise.

4. *What's the best way to contact a search firm?*

I have two thoughts here. *First*, if you already know someone in the search business, contact them. That person may be willing to invest more time in you and your search than someone you don't know. In this case, I suggest a call, followed by your resume. Use the call to find out the kinds of searches they are currently involved with; try to assess the kinds of candidates they're looking for. Then you can customize your resume to better match those assignments. If you can't uncover details, send your resume and say in the cover letter that you will follow up in five working days to see what the next steps are.

Second, plan a different approach if you don't have a contact at a search firm. In this case, mail your resume, along with a cover letter that summarizes your major qualifications. At this point most job-search consultants advise you not to follow up by phone. The recruiter is interested only in candidates who fit their current openings. I agree, especially if you are sending information to a national or international search firm. Don't risk alienating recruiters who may find an opening for you later by taking up their time now.

I think you can plan a different approach if you are contacting a small search firm – with one to

64

three or four recruiters. I believe in this case it IS okay to follow up your resume and cover letter with a phone call. You have a better chance of establishing a relationship with someone from a small firm than you do a large firm. It's my experience that people in smaller search firms are more likely to take the time with you on the phone.

5. *Should I work only with a retained search firm or also with contingency firms?*

For people early in their careers and for most mid-level positions, contingency firms are more likely to help. Retained search firms tend to handle the senior positions. One caution: If you are employed but are searching confidentially, be careful not to contact any retained search organization your employer uses. It has happened, with embarrassing results.

6. *What should a cover letter include?*

First, always include a cover letter. Keep it short and to the point; list any specific qualifications you feel match up with the position you are looking for. You want to quickly capture the reader's attention and clearly communicate your experience, accomplishments and employment history. (Refer to Chapter 5 on cover letters.)

7. *I never hear back from a recruiter. How long should I wait before I call them back?*

This question gets at the heart of the problem with search firms and recruiters. You won't get a call unless you "fit" a specific position. In fact, recruiters may forget you are in their database until your file comes up on a computer match. Anticipate and expect recruiters won't call – unless they have a possible match.

An excellent reference guide to executive search firms around the country is *The Directory of Executive Recruiters 1998; 27th Edition.* Commonly referred to as the Red Book, it's a listing of more

than 3500 search firms, comprehensively cross-indexed by management function, geography and industry. Also identified in the 1998 edition are more than 10,000 executive recruiters and their areas of specialty. This reference is updated annually. You'll find it in any library or in the career resource center of most community colleges and universities.

A final thought on search firms and placement services – use them, but don't rely on them as your only approach. You are releasing control over part of your job search, but you could be in the nine percent of people who get a job this way. So you don't want to miss out.

Using the Internet

The Internet provides a very interesting job-search alternative. However, its strength is its weakness. I'm excited about its potential because of the vast number of opportunities and the access to information it provides. At the same time, I'm concerned because of its vastness. I'm not convinced that it's as effective as some people say it is in generating quality job leads or interviews.

How the Internet works

Essentially, the Internet provides three ways to search for job leads:

1. General job-search sites;
2. Company web sites; and
3. Research sites.

General job-search sites.

These are the so-called "big boards" which offer hundreds, if not thousands, of job listings and large resume banks. At most of these sites, applicants can post their resume (commonly referred to as a profile) for free. Essentially, when you post your profile to one of these "big boards," you're adding yourself to a large databank. Companies and recruiters pay to access these databanks, searching for candidates who match the criteria for open positions. Make sure you can update and edit your profile once it's listed with a big board.

I'm not convinced that big boards are effective. Posting your resume is another opportunity to circulate your resume, however, control is the issue. Who makes the decisions in this case? It's the employers or recruiters who pay to search the big board databank – not you. They select those profiles that best match their criteria. You don't plan an active role. In fact, just as with executive search firms, you won't even know if you're being considered until someone calls – if they call.

Company web sites.

Company web sites are an excellent source of information. Many post job openings. The value to you is that these sites also provide useful information about the company. Not only will you find detailed information about the position but you'll find information about its culture, mission, products, services, location, etc. In addition, you may find contact names and phone numbers. Use this data to make a personal contact with a company that has a job you're interested in.

The benefit to company web sites is that you keep some control of your job search. You decide to apply for a position based on information you collect. A caution about information found on company web sites: it can be biased and sugar-coated. This is why a company web site is a good place to begin your research of that company. Further research may be required to get a complete understanding of the company. This is why the research web sites are useful.

Research sites.

Research web sites allow you to get objective information on a company. Typically, these sites provide a company profile, list of officers, a stock chart and latest financial figures. They provide links to other sites where you can get other information like stories written about the company.

Making your resume "net-compatible"

With each web site, you'll use their profile format to input your resume. Your goal is to provide enough information to be "searchable" – ensure the best possible probability of a potential employer's requirements. Typical profiles request:

- Personal information;
- Professional history;
- Professional skills;
- Career goals or objectives;
- Specialty areas;
- Academic history including degrees, certifications, associations, memberships and licenses;
- Personal preferences including location;
- Position preferences; and
- Languages spoken.

Each profile has its own format. You can't customize your information for a particular employer. However, in most web sites you can edit and update your information.

The benefits

Employers benefit from web sites because they can uniformly profile applicants, automate their candidate selection process, and build a databank of potential candidates to select from. It allows them to search a huge pool of candidates – many more than they would be able to if they used traditional methods.

The benefit to applicants is not as clear. I don't think it is an effective tool for applicants. Most literature exaggerates its effectiveness. Pick up any article on job web sites and it leads you to believe all you have to do is fill out the profile information for that web site, submit it, and sit back and wait for the calls to roll in. That's exactly what you'll do – wait, and wait, and wait for the calls. Who makes the decisions here – not you. It's the employer who has paid a fee to use the databank as a source of candidates. What are the chances that your profile (not customized) will catch the eye of an employer when it is one of 150,000 profiles? Slim, at best!

Instead, I suggest using the Internet as a resource and research tool to inform and significantly expand your networking. It's a wealth of information about industries, companies, trends, locales, etc. Use your creativity to uncover ideas and possible leads you never dreamed of.

What are the web sites?

There are dozens of career-related web sites on the Internet. New ones are added daily; some disappear. The few I've listed below were valid sites as of Spring 1998. Continue to browse the Web for new and improved sites. Your best strategy is to test each major site and stick with those that return the most pertinent job leads.

Explore these health care related sites.

1. Medical Group Management Association Placement Intranet (http://www.MGMA. com). This is a placement service where applicants are matched against available positions. Applicants pay a small fee to be included in the databank. Employers pay to list job vacancies and to access the databank. MGMA alerts the applicant of a match, then, if interested, the applicant contacts the employer.

NOTES

2. Healthcare Financial Management Association (http://www.hfma.org). Their home page includes a link to jobs and classified ads. These are health care financial management related positions available throughout the country. The list is updated.

3. JobSpan by EthoSolutions (http://www.job-span.com). This web site specializes in health care positions. Applicants create an on-line profile, a resume, using the JobSpan profiling software. Applicants can search open positions by state or position type. Simply click on a position to submit your JobSpan profile. Applicants can update profiles anytime. Employers submit position descriptions for open jobs indicating qualifications. Applicant and position qualifications are compared – "hits" are based on matching applicants.

Popular job-search sites (sometimes referred to as "big-boards")

1. The Monster Board (http://www.monster.com). This is a service that lists thousands of jobs from more than 4000 companies from various industries including health care. Jobs range from entry-level to executive management positions. New jobs are posted daily and can be accessed 24 hours a day, seven days a week. You can search by specific criteria such as location, job function or industry.

2. CareerPath (http://www.careerpath.com). This site contains classified job listings from dozens of US daily newspapers and has an easily executed search engine. It may be the best overall site for general job hunting. Approximately 250,000 jobs are listed. You can focus your search by region or industry.

3. Career Mosaic (http://www.careermosaic.com). This site typically has over 70,000 jobs listed. Its services are free to job seekers. You can scan the listings and even post your resume

for potential employers to see. It provides industry-specific listings.

4. NationJob Network (http://www.nation-job.com). You can enter your personal profile of your ideal job – location, salary and industry. Provide your e-mail address and wait for appropriate listings to be sent to you.

Widescale sites

1. Hover's OnLine (http://www.hovers.com). This site offers profiles and financial data on more than 12,000 public and private companies worldwide. It provides links to other free sites where you can explore even more.

2. Job-Smart (http://www.jobsmart.org). This site offers a warehouse of salary surveys. It details more than 150 salary surveys for various industries, compiled by professional organizations and recruiters.

Other useful web sites

1) Resume Bank (http://www.resumail.com). This is a resource employers use when searching for qualified applicants.

2) Yahoo search engine (http://www. yahoo.com/ Business/ Employment/). This is Yahoo's gateway to employment-related web sites.

This list is small. There are hundreds of others. Start searching. I'd like to hear if you find others you feel are worthwhile and useful.

The Internet is an excellent source of ideas and information which will help in your job search. Use it to expand your job-search networking opportunities. Think of it as just one tool in your job-search tool kit. It's just one method to make yourself known to employers. My advice: don't make it your **only** tool to generate interviews.

Remember, you can't control who sees your profile. Employers who review your resume on-line make decisions based on the information in that profile. If there's a match with their needs – great, they'll contact you. If not – no call. There is no way to customize your profile. Don't expect your resume, when posted to an Internet databank, to generate a lot of calls. Your Internet time is best used uncovering information that leads to networking opportunities and face-to-face contacts. Your best chance for interviews will come from using this approach.

Responding to ads in newspapers and professional trade journals

Usually, classified ads are the first place people turn to begin their job search. It's a good source but remember that, statistically, only about 10 percent of jobs come through classified ads. The percentage increases if you target positions advertised in a professional trade journal such as the *MGM Update* (the monthly newsletter of the Medical Group Management Association) or the *HFM Journal* (the monthly newsletter of the Healthcare Financial Management Association). Make sure ads comprise only about 10 percent of your job-search efforts.

Thoughts about ads

1. Ads contain valuable information you can use to customize a cover letter and decide how to rank the accomplishment statements on your resume. For example, let's look at the following ad that appeared in a past issue of the *MGM Update*:

Clinic Manager

A 12-physician multi-speciality group practice is seeking a manager with at least 5 years of group practice management experience, strong financial skills and excellent interpersonal and communication skills. Practice includes a staff of nine physician assistants and four satellite clinics.

Position requires a minimum of a BS degree in business or health care administration with a master's degree preferred. Experience with managed care contracting and capitation essential. Salary negotiable.

Qualified candidates please send resume with salary history to:
Dr. Jim Jones, Chairman
Anywhere USA Clinic, P.C.
PO Box XXXX
Anywhere, USA, 11111

Here's how you would use the information in this ad to customize both your cover letter and resume. Read through the ad again and underline the critical information.

You may have underlined:

- Five years experience;
- Multi-speciality group;
- Management experience;
- Four satellite clinics;
- BS degree or Master's degree preferred; and
- Managed care or capitation experience essential.

Having identified the important information found in the ad, you can now customize your cover letter and resume to match any or all of these requirements. Learn to read all classified ads with a critical eye. (Refer to Chapter 5 for details on how to customize your cover letters to the requirements you find in classified ads.)

2.   Look for ads that include the name of the organization or a contact person. This is very valuable information. If this much detail is provided, you have a chance to collect more information before you prepare and send your cover letter and resume. Take advantage of the opportunity to call the name (or organization) listed and ask questions about the position. For example, you might ask about the type of managed care or capitation contracts its clinic handles. Or you might find out the extent of the services offered at each satellite clinic. You will find out very valuable information and be able to customize your cover letter in even more detail.

There's another benefit. You can now send your material to a person who will remember you. You can open your cover letter with a statement that reminds them of your phone discussion. They will remember you.

3.   Some employers will use blind ads. These are ads that do not list a company or contact person. They may list only a PO Box number or their address. If it is a PO Box, it is nearly impossible to find out who the hiring organization is. If only an address is listed, it does increase your chances of locating the name of the organization. All it takes is sleuthing and a few phone calls to locate a company name. Employers use blind ads as a way to gather a list of qualified candidates without identifying their organization. Be careful that the blind ad is not for a position at your company or for your job. This has happened before.

Making "cold" calls – a waste of your time

Don't waste your time and effort on cold calling or broadcasting your resume to 75-100 potential names in one mailing. It doesn't work. Less than one percent of jobs are found this way. Your letters usually end up in the trash. Not many of my clients have tried mass mailings. One who did said he had sent out more than 125 letters and resumes to medical groups and hospitals in areas of the country where he wanted to relocate. The result – two responses and those were, "We received your letter and resume and don't have any positions at this time, but have put your resume on file for six months." He never heard from them again. As you can see, most organizations don't even make an effort to respond.

Relying on old-fashioned luck

You may think I am joking when I mention luck. I'm not. I can't tell you how many clients I work with who initially struggle against the amount of work and effort it takes to prepare for and do a job search in today's environment. A common feeling is that, in the past, "jobs have always found me" or "I've never had to make the effort to find a job; someone, usually a headhunter, has always called me." I call this approach LUCK – being in the right place at the right time. And, given the environment that you find yourself in today, the chance of this happening with you is low – I never say never, because there is that slim chance that someone will call you *out of the blue.* If it happens with you – great! Chances are it won't. It is up to you to create the environment in which those calls start coming. Don't wait for them!

NOTES

Take charge of your selling tools I: sharpen your resume

Resume dilemma

For years, poor resumes have caused people to miss out on jobs they want and often deserve. You may one of these people. Or you may be a college graduate just starting into the job market and wondering how to apply for a position or what to include on a resume that will increase your chances of receiving a call requesting an interview. Or you may be a professional with several years of group practice or hospital experience seeking advancement or change.

Like most of us, you may be bewildered by the quantity of "advice" in textbooks, pamphlets, and newspaper or journal articles – much of it contradictory or counterproductive. Browse your local bookstore section on careers and you will find 40 - 50 different books on resumes and resume writing with just as many describing cover letters. Where do you begin? Whose format do you use; what will the resume reader read? Is one format better than the others? All good questions but, unfortunately, questions without one right answer.

Should you or shouldn't you open with a job-objective statement? Should you or shouldn't you use off-white or colored paper? Is a certain type font better than others? What kinds of verbs should start the "bullet" statements on your resume? Should you even use bullets or are paragraphs more appropriate? How do you include 15 years of experience in a one-or two-page resume? How should you organize a cover letter? Do you even need a cover letter?

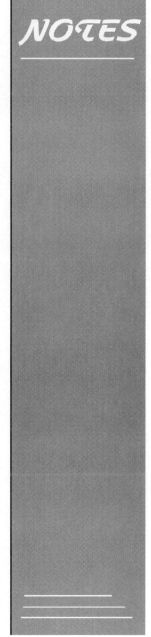

NOTES

Actually, most of these questions deal with minor issues – what might be called the mechanics of job search. There are more critical questions you must address before you even think about questions like these. In fact, resumes (and writing about them) suffer from restrictions that rest in the very name itself: "resume" derived from the French *résumer*, meaning "to summarize, as in one's qualifications and experience."

Your resume is really a proposal

We need to recognize first that resumes must not merely summarize – whether they be filled with details marked by dates and job titles or, as has more recently become popular, with related functions and accomplishments. Instead, consider a resume a proposal document in which you're proposing yourself as a solution to a prospective employer's problem and need.

If you accept that resumes are personal proposals, certain principles become evident. For example, the correct model for resumes is the informal proposal, which strongly resembles an effective marketing sales letter. To evaluate a resume, you should apply the same basic standards that apply to writing a proposal:

• Does the resume respond to the employer's specific needs?

• Do you, as the writer, demonstrate ability, and especially, effectiveness?

• Does your resume emphasize results that motivate the hiring manager or human-resources representative to contact you for an interview?

• Does your resume demonstrate your efficiency and accountabilities?

• Will the person reviewing your resume determine that you may provide the best value for the money (salary)?

- Will the hiring manager determine that because of your background and experience, you would be the best person to help him or her deal with the organization's needs, to help solve their problems?

Proposals don't merely inform, they persuade! Thus, your goal in preparing and using a resume is to get the reader to do or act rather than merely to absorb information or to think. You want readers to act in your favor. Motivate them by customizing your entire presentation packet to the specific needs of the reader.

To customize your resume to the needs of the organization and the reader, you first have to know those needs. Second, you must show how your past experience makes you the ideal candidate. Organizational needs are usually stated as requirements or qualifications desired. Use accomplishments, rather than skill or responsibility statements, because employers are interested in results – what you can do for them. Abilities, interests and previous responsibilities may not motivate them to call. Asserting you can do something asks your reader to have faith in you; showing that you've done something – and stressing how that result matches the employer's needs – convinces the reader to act in your favor. Favorable actions translate into getting the face-to-face job interview. Getting the first job interview may lead to a second interview, which may eventually translate into a job offer.

But it's not this simple!

I've already stated that your resume is a persuasive document, a proposal, in which you are motivating the reader into action – to schedule a face-to-face interview or a screening interview phone call. Here's the catch! Your resume must grab the reader's attention, to persuade the reader to pick up the phone and call – **in 15 seconds.** Yes, that's right, 15 seconds to persuade the reader to action.

NOTES

Key Point

- You must grab the reader's attention in 15 seconds.

Hiring managers who screen resumes make their first decision to screen in or screen out in 15 seconds. If your resume is screened in, it's put in a pile for review in more detail at a later time. In-depth reviews and calls for interviews come from this stack.

So, how do you increase your chances of getting into the screened-in pile? Although no technique is 100 percent fool proof, you can present yourself in a way that persuades readers that your experience and background – your accomplishments – match their needs. Your goal is to make them want to find out more about you and your background.

Your strategy

It sounds like an impossible mission, especially when you think of how many people – all with comparable skills, background and experience – are applying for the same position. Forget the rule-of-thumb that says you MUST keep your resume to one or two pages. It's impossible to summarize all your experience and accomplishments in two pages and still hope to somehow match the interests and needs of the reader. I've seen hundreds of resumes where the individual has tried everything possible to keep their resume to one page, even going to a 10 or 8 point type. Some resumes have had such small type that I almost felt the need to use a magnifying glass. When asked about the small type, the individual said he had been told to keep it to one page. To meet that goal, he had to use small type to get 10 years of experience on one page. Don't be concerned about length – it's the quality that counts.

Now that I've put that notion to rest, here's what I suggest you do. From now on, consider your cover letter the first page of your resume. Remember, your job is to capture the reader's interest in 15 seconds. With 15 seconds to work with, readers have enough time to skim your cover letter and the top half of page two (the first page of your resume). That's all they see for the screen-in/screen-out decision. All other information is backup and supporting material readers review because they want to.

Here's a decision point – what information should you include on the first one and one-half pages? What information should you leave out? This decision is aided by the research you've done on that particular job opening, the needs and requirements.

With this framework clearly in mind, your next step is to review your resume database and decide which accomplishments will provide the best or closest MATCH to the identified needs (stated requirements and qualifications) of that organization.

Using your resume database

I introduced the resume database in Chapter 3. Now you use it.

Whenever we think of preparing and using a resume, we think just that – to prepare and send our ONE resume. Typically we use a one-size-fits-all resume for every situation. Now, ask yourself a question, "How effectively will my one-size-fits-all resume match the unique needs and requirements of each job I apply? Will it persuade someone from a single-specialty medical group of seven physicians as well as someone from a 35-physician, multi-specialty group?" The answer – probably not. A one-size-fits-all resume is not an effective self-marketing tool.

Customize your cover letter and resume for each opportunity. Select the information from your resume database that best matches the unique needs and requirements of each position. Each time you apply for a position or give your resume to someone as background – it MUST be customized and tailored for that situation.

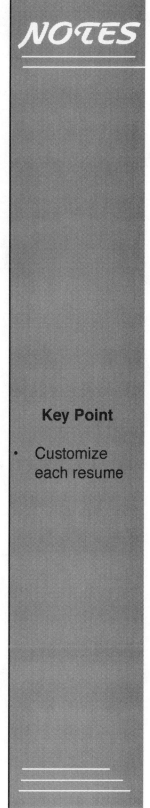

NOTES

Key Point

- Customize each resume

Don't worry, customizing is not a time-consuming job. Keep a template on your computer along with your resume database. You'll find that approximately 70 - 75 percent of your resume doesn't change. The other 25 - 30 percent will persuade readers to *screen you in.*

Customize in several ways. You can:

- Include accomplishment statements from your database that closely match the reader's needs;

- Prioritize your accomplishment statements – list them in a way that sets them apart from your other statements; and

- Include more detailed information with accomplishments that match the requirements. You may end up with accomplishment statements that are in outline form – one main point followed by four or five detailed subpoints. I provide examples later in this chapter.

Always customize every cover letter. Use your best accomplishment statements in your cover letter. Give readers an early indication about how well your background matches with their needs. Let them know in the first two or three seconds that you are someone they should talk to. Repeat these same accomplishment statements in your resume.

What do I include in my database?

In one word: Everything! Every project, assignment, task, accomplishment you can think of from your professional and personal life; include volunteer activities. Don't hold back. You never know when you may want to use an example in a resume, a marketing letter, or an interview. It's easier to choose from information on a database rather than try to think of specific examples on the spur of the moment.

Tips and tactics for fine-tuning your resume

Here are some important tips to consider when preparing your database and customizing resumes.

Length

Don't limit yourself to one, two or three pages. Including cover letter, your resume can be longer. As you know, it's physically impossible to summarize five, ten, even 15 years of experience on one or two pages. So don't! Once readers have screened in your resume, they are more likely to want to read on – to find out more detail about you because they are interested, not because they are still trying to find a reason to screen you in or out. They are motivated to take the time to read further.

Layout

Your layout should provide for quick and easy scanning. Organize your information to help readers find your key accomplishments quickly and easily. Don't overload pages with long, single-spaced paragraphs. Use short paragraphs with bullets to highlight specific facts or information. Leave white space so it's visually pleasing to the reader's eye. Most readers won't take time to hunt for information– you have to help them. If the person screening can't quickly determine there's a match, he or she will simply move to the next resume. Yours will have been eliminated.

Review the following two examples. Notice the difference. Which example might help the reader find key information? Which format do you like? Do you now use either format? Could you revise your resume to make it more "reader friendly?"

John Smith
123 Roadway St.
Anywhere, CA 99999
Home: (303) 555 - 1212

Professional Summary

More than 15 years of progressive administrative and management experience in both single-specialty and multi-specialty medical groups. Expertise includes handling medical group mergers and acquisitions, facility design and construction, acquisition and development of ancillary services, managed care contracting and development of an ambulatory surgery center/endoscopy lab. Successfully led the merger of several small practices totaling 24 physicians to form Executive Medical Group, P.C., the Middle States largest physician-owned medical group.

Administrator/CEO   **1995 - Present**
Executive Medical Group, P.C.

Initially accepted the position of Administrator/CEO of the Midtown Orthopedic Associates, P.C., a five-physician practice with its own physical therapy unit. Proceeded to acquire the Center for Work Enhancement and then merge with a four-person anesthesiology group and a neurologist to form Executive Medical Group, P.C.

In 1996, was selected to lead the process of a merger of five practices representing 35 physicians into Executive Medical Group, P.C. The merger was effective mid-1996 and has subsequently grown into a 55-physician, 25-extender organization.

Accomplishments in addition to the merger itself include the addition of 20 new physicians and five new specialties; the acquisition of imaging services including MRI and ultrasound; development and construction of two new primary care locations; managed care organization negotiations resulting in several exclusive arrangements including one with Primeria Healthcare Network; the integration and consolidation of operational and financial policies and procedures; and consolidation to one professional liability insurance carrier resulting in an increase in benefits while saving approximately $100,000 annually in premiums.

Example 2: Bullet format and layout:

John Smith
123 Roadway St.
Anywhere, CA 99999
Home: (303) 555 - 1212

Professional Summary

More than 15 years of progressive administrative and management experience in both single-specialty and multi-specialty medical groups. Expertise includes handling medical group mergers and acquisitions, facility design and construction, acquisition and development of ancillary services, managed care contracting and development of an ambulatory surgery center/endoscopy lab. Successfully led the merger of several small practices totaling 24 physicians to form Executive Medical Group, P.C., the Middle States largest physician-owned medical group.

Administrator/CEO   **1995 - Present**
Executive Medical Group, P.C.

- Planned and led the process of a merger of five practices representing 35 physicians into Executive Medical Group, P.C. The merger was effective mid-1996 and has subsequently grown into a 55-physician, 25 extender organization.

- Recruited 20 new physicians and five new specialties for the group including . . . .

- Demonstrated the need for and acquired MRI and ultrasound equipment.

- Developed and oversaw the construction of two new primary care locations.

- Negotiated the first managed care contracts that resulted in several exclusive arrangements including one with Primaria Healthcare Network.

- Consolidated all operational and financial policies and procedures into one easy-to-use reference manual.

- Consolidated multiple liability insurance policies with one carrier resulting in an increase in benefits while saving approximately $100,000 in annual premiums.

These two samples contain identical information. Is the second example easier to read? Why? If you were screening this resume, would you be able to "find" relevant information more easily in the second example?

Notice the use of white space. Ask yourself how that makes it easier to read and pick out the key points. Then look at the first example, in which the information is crowded onto the page. Look back to the Professional Summary statement in example 2. It's a bit cumbersome for someone to read. How might you use lists or bullets to make it easier to pull out important facts and details?

Here's one way to present the professional summary:

John Smith
123 Roadway St.
Anywhere, CA 99999
Home: (303) 555 -1212

Professional Summary

More than 15 years of progressive administrative and management experience in both single-specialty and multi-specialty medical groups including:

- Handling medical group mergers and acquisitions.
- Managed care contracting.
- Acquired and developed
  ancillary services.
- Facility design and construction.
- Developed ambulatory surgery center/ endoscopy lab.

Successfully led the merger of several small practices, totaling 24 physicians, to form Executive Medical Group, P.C., the Middle States' largest physician-owned medical group.

What do you think? Do bullets make it easier to find information? Can you pick out the key qualifications any quicker? The last sentence of this summary is an example of customizing a resume. If the position you are applying for requires merger and integration experience, and you have that experience, use it in your professional summary. Move it "up-front." Repeat by using the same statement as one of your accomplishment statements in the body of the resume. If it's not a critical need, place that statement only in the body of the resume as a bulleted accomplishment.

Active writing style

Language used in your resume must be crisp, succinct, yet personal. The words you use must illustrate results through activity and energy. Look for the phrases that convey personal energy and commitment. Readers will tune in to an active writing style. Language helps your resume make a positive impression in the first 15 seconds.

Here's an example.

A typical accomplishment statement may read:

• *Successfully planned and opened four satellite offices in just nine months.*

The statement is descriptive and communicates the action taken; it describes the scope of the project; and it implies a result or outcome. However, a statement like this begs to be expanded. People screening this resume and reading this statement may ask themselves, "I wonder what she did when she did that? I would like to know more." This is especially true if this organization plans to open satellite offices soon.

Here's how it could be expanded using a more active and descriptive writing style:

- *Successfully planned and opened four satellite offices in just nine months:*

  * *Proposed and completed a three-year planning and building project that included adding 25,000 square feet of space in the four satellite centers and renovating 15,000 square feet into a state-of-the-art facility that helped improve patient access to services throughout five counties.*
  * *Opened the four physician offices on schedule and 20 percent under budget.*
  * *Advertised for, interviewed, and hired more than 25 employees during the expansion period, including nursing and medical extender staff.*
  * *Evaluated three computer-billing, accounting and management-reporting systems with recommendations on the process to replace existing systems.*

Note the use of action and results-oriented words like *successfully, opened, under budget, evaluated*. These words imply energy and activity on your part. They get attention. Use them to help stimulate interest in you and your accomplishments. They may motivate the reader to "screen you in." By the way, these are also examples of key words that might be "picked up" if your resume was electronically screened. You'll find more on the use of electronically screened resumes and using resumes on the Internet later in this chapter.

Avoid using "I"

Avoid repeated use of "I" at the beginning of sentences and accomplishment statements. Here's one example from a client's professional summary that contains too many "I's." As you read it, think how the use of "I's" makes it more difficult to read.

I have 15 years experience in the health care field primarily in the fiscal and administrative areas of hospitals and multi-specialty groups. Fiscally, I have had responsibility as an assistant comptroller of a medical center, then I was an assistant administrator of a for-profit hospital. Most recently, I am administrator of a multi-specialty group . . . . . .

Notice the use of "I's" in the statement. Do they make it hard for the reader to focus on this person's background? Here's how this paragraph could be written.

> *"Extensive career in hospital and multi-specialty medical group administration with steady progression to higher levels of management. As administrator, provided leadership in administrative and fiscal areas, human resources, growth and managing physician services, securing and maintaining regulatory compliance."*

What's different? Does it read any easier? How might you re-write it? Notice the crispness of the statement. It's to the point, summarizing skills and experience in areas that are of interest to the reader. Review your own material. Do you include too many I's? If so, how could you revise it? Be creative.

Proofread

There is only one rule when it comes to typos: NO typos or errors of any kind – period! Meticulously read and re-read your written work. Ask someone unfamiliar with the material to proofread. It's easy to miss the small typos. For example, *your* instead of *you*, and *in* instead of *if* or *is* are common errors and very easy to make. It's these little errors your computer spell-check won't find and you may miss in proof reading. Someone else may find them.

What other words are easily transposed and used incorrectly? Do you have any hidden misspelled words in your resume? You'd better check – one or two could be laying there waiting for a screener to uncover them. And check again and again, and again.

Use quality paper

Many so-called experts suggest using different colored paper or a unique type style to make your resume and cover letter stand out. I Don't! Use a high quality, white paper stock. Consider your cover or marketing letter and resume a professional document – a proposal. You probably haven't seen any proposals printed on colored or tinted paper? Unless it's for an advertising agency. Paper color or fancy type won't capture the kind of attention you want. Information captures attention. It's how you plan and lay out your document; how you craft accomplishment statements; it's what you say – that's how you capture interest.

Don't type-set your cover letter and resume. Don't forget – customize, customize, customize. Even if you only change 5 percent, that 5 percent may be the difference in capturing the reader's attention.

Use a laser or inkjet printer. This type of printer produces clean, crisp looking documents, whereas materials from a dot-matrix printer may leave smudges and smears. Laser- or inkjet-printed materials get attention.

Clients often ask if they should use color instead of bold face on their heading. I don't recommend using color. It's **what** you say, not how you say it that gets attention. A screener may say, "Look at the color. How nice. But what can this person really do for me?"

Choosing a font

Select a font that is professional and easy to read. New Times Roman or Arial are excellent types if you use a PC. Macintosh users will find Palatino an excellent choice. Consider Arial Bold for subheadings. Don't use fancy type; remember, your resume and cover letter should be a proposal document.

Faxing resumes

Most organizations and groups accept faxed resumes. In fact, most classified ads include a fax number. Whenever you fax a cover letter/resume, ALWAYS mail a clean copy of the same material. In the faxed cover letter, tell the reader you're following up this fax by mailing a clean copy. This serves two purposes: First, fax machines may not reproduce a crisp, clean copy. Margins may be cut off or a page may not cleanly transmit. I've received many faxes where the information in the center of the page is squeezed together and unreadable. Second, sending a follow-up copy allows you to put your name (and material) in front of the company and contact person a second time. It never hurts to remind the organization of you!

What not to include in your resume

This is simple – don't include any information that could potentially screen you out. Remember, your resume has only one purpose – to get an interview. It's a judgment call because you'll never be 100-percent clear what information might screen you out. Advice I give clients is this – if you have any thought that the information doesn't apply – leave it out.

Here are the general categories of information to omit:

- Salary history/requirements;
- Reasons for leaving your previous job;
- Availability date;
- Location preference;
- Resume preparation date; and
- Personal information about your family or your photo.

Here's why.

Salary history/requirements

Never include salary figures on a resume or cover letter. Once you do, the hiring organization is in a position to make a screen in or out decision before contacting you. Companies ask for salary information for only one reason – so they have data with which to decide for themselves if you fit *their* salary structure.

Here's what can happen when you provide salary information – notice that two of the three are negative:

1. If you indicate a salary requirement that is below their range – two things can happen and both are negative. They may decide you don't have the experience or background. The result: You're screened out without an interview and a chance to demonstrate your abilities. The other possibility is that you may be screened in because they could make an offer that is below their salary budget. Result: You lose again with a lower salary, even though you received an offer;

2. If you indicate a salary requirement that is higher than their range, they may screen you out because you're "overqualified." If you are perceived as "being overqualified," it's usually interpreted as, "This person will be bored in six months and may move on. We won't take the chance"; or

3. Your salary requirement happens to fall within their range. Then salary isn't an issue, and you will be screened in or out based on other information in your cover letter or resume.

Here are two sentences to consider using instead of a dollar amount. I've had many hiring managers tell me that statements like these are acceptable:

- "Your ad requested salary requirements. Before providing a meaningful salary requirement, I would like to discuss the duties and responsibilities presented by the job in greater detail"; or

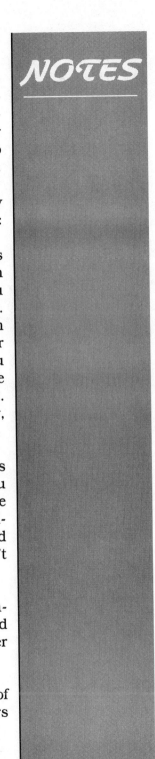

NOTES

- "Your ad requested salary information. My salary history has paralleled the level of responsibility and authority of previous positions. My salary requirements are flexible depending on the responsibilities and advancement opportunities within your organization."

(Refer to Chapter 5 for more information on referencing salary requirements in cover letters.)

Reasons for leaving your previous job

Wait until the face-to-face interview to talk about the reasons you are changing jobs or have left your previous job. Anyone reviewing your written material may make an erroneous assumption based on what or how you state your reasons. For example, you could very honestly state that "my job was eliminated due to cutbacks in the workforce." This could be true but you do not know how this statement may be interrupted by the screener. You don't know how someone may react to this statement. Some will read it for what it is; others may read more into it than is necessary and decide to eliminate your application. Again, a negative decision was made for you, by someone else. The decision was out of your control.

Available date

Indicating an available date can be interpreted negatively – people may think you're someone who is panicked or desperate for a job, even though you are trying to communicate you want to be responsive to their needs and work with their timetable. Start dates are always negotiated later in the hiring process.

Location preference

Don't worry about location this early in the search process. Your goal is to get the face-to-face interview. Indicating that you "want" or "require" a certain site may screen you out early in the process. If you know the organization would require you to relocate, you can decide to discontinue. It's your decision, made based on your own personal needs.

Some feel that waiting until you are well into the hiring process to tell the organization you will not relocate and therefore will not accept an offer when you know this earlier may be unethical. I suggest it isn't. Here's why. You never know when you might learn new information about the company that could change your mind. It could be that dream job you have been looking for and after more consideration decide that relocation is ok. Maybe, during the interviews you found out the relocation would be temporary. Or maybe you uncovered another job in that company that wouldn't require you to relocate. Never close off options until you are sure you have **all** the information.

Date you prepared the resume

Your customized cover letter will include a date. That date will be enough. Don't date your resume.

Personal information about your family or your photo

Information about your family, hobbies or personal photo doesn't help you get a face-to-face interview. It's extraneous information people must sift through to find what's important.

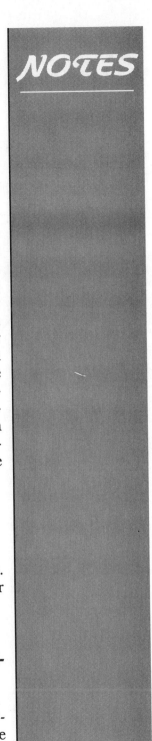

97

Most hiring managers won't take the time to read through personal information. When included at the front of your resume, it may screen you out. Focusing on your personal data first also may indicate to readers that you haven't prepared your materials adequately or that you may not have the necessary experience and background to be a realistic candidate for the position.

Resume formats

What if I were to suggest that your resume format is not important. I will say it – the format is not critical. I know this is contrary to everything you've heard or read. Books have been published describing resumes that *knock 'em dead*. That's usually what happens, a resume literally knocks 'em dead or at least *puts 'em asleep.*

There are three generally accepted formats: 1) chronological; 2) functional; and 3) the marketing letter. You've heard experts recommend the chronological format and discourage the functional format. I don't agree with this argument. I suggest selecting the format that BEST fits each different situation. Remember, your objective is to demonstrate how your experience matches the needs of that particular opportunity. In one case, you may decide the chronological format is best. In another case, a marketing letter is appropriate. Likewise, there will be times when a functional format is best because listing accomplishments by major function will get attention quicker.

Your objective, in 15 seconds, is to capture the reader's interest – motivate the person to pick up the phone and call. Choose a style or format that best accomplishes this objective. Fit the format to your needs; don't fit your needs to a format.

Chronological format

The chronological form is the more widely used and accepted format. It's typically used when someone's career consists of an uninterrupted succession of positions and is progressing in a well-defined path toward a career goal. In this format your most recent work experience is listed first, then continue backward in time listing previous work history in reverse order.

Using the chronological format

The major blocks of information commonly found in a chronological format are:

- Heading;
- Objective statement;
- Professional summary statement;
- Professional experience listed in chronological order beginning with your most recent and moving backward until you've covered your entire work history;
- Education/certifications; and
- Related professional information.

A detailed description of each section follows.

Headings

This is a critical piece of information for the reader, yet it's also an area where mistakes are often made. Headings should be easy for the reader to quickly find the most important information of all – your name and telephone number. Include your name, mailing address, phone and fax numbers. Here are some tips to make your heading easy for the reader to read and use.

Your name. Simple enough, yes, but even here you might cause confusion. Always use the first name you most frequently go by. For example, my given name is Harold but I always go by Hal. In

Key Point

- Fit the format to your needs.

fact, the only time I use Harold is on legal documents like driver's license, insurance policies, etc. I never use Harold in my day-to-day activity, so I use Hal in my heading. Using Harold may confuse the person calling when I answer the phone "Hello, this is Hal . . . ." and the caller is expecting Harold. My voice-mail message may also cause the caller confusion because I use Hal, not Harold. When callers are expecting a "Harold," but voice mail indicates "Hal," they may not be 100 percent sure they have reached the correct phone number.

Some people feel they should use their formal name on the resume; I don't.

Your address. Clients often ask if they should use their home address, or if it is it more professional to use an office address. Use your home address. You don't want job-search mail coming to your work address. Be sure the address information is correct. This in one place where a typo can sneak in, and you might miss it. I've seen many resumes with the wrong street address – where a number was transposed. I've also seen examples where a client has moved but forgotten to change the address on the resume. Make sure your zip code is correct.

Phone and fax numbers. Always identify numbers as phone – home, work and fax. Here's some tips on using your home phone number: 1) You MUST have either voice mail or a home answering machine. Never miss a call; and 2) Always use a professional sounding message – one that is direct and specifically identifies you. This lets callers know that they have reached the correct number. NEVER use those prerecorded messages with talking pets, 5-year olds, or Louis Armstrong singing your message. Those funny messages may get a laugh, but if you are expecting prospective employers to call your home, use a professional message.

Don't use a work number. If you do, be 100 percent confident that no one except you will ever
answer that phone. If there is **any** chance that
someone in your office would answer your phone
in your absence, don't use it. Only use your work
phone number in messages that go directly to a
private voice-message mail box and you are the
only one who picks up those messages. I've seen
too many examples in which a confidential job
search has become "office gossip" when an unsus-
pecting office assistant picked up a message and
then quite innocently mentioned it to someone
else over lunch.

Make your heading readable. Here are two examples of headings I feel are ineffective because they
hide your information; they make it difficult for
someone to quickly find your phone number:

Example 1:

Janet Smith

1111 South Jackson Street	(303) 555 - 1212 (Home)
Denver, CO 80012	303) 555 - 1213 (Fax)

Example 2:

Janet Smith

1111 South Jackson Street	(303) 555 - 1212 (Home)
Denver, CO 80012	(303) 555 - 1213 (Fax)

What makes these two examples confusing and
hard to read? Sometimes, clients feel a need to
add design that doesn't provide any benefit. It
only makes it more difficult for the reader to find
the information. If your format appears confusing, it is. Your goal is to provide information
about yourself that is easy to read and easy to
understand. Easy-to-read fonts are critical in

NOTES

your heading. Don't get fancy in your heading by hiding critical information above or below lines, boxes, or with any other designs. Don't use those script type fonts like London, Los Angeles or Zapf Chancery. Present your data clearly – centered on the top of the page. For example:

Janet Smith
1111 South Jackson Street
Denver, CO 80012
(303) 555 - 1212 (Home)
(303) 555 - 1213 (Fax)

Objective statement

Consider an objective statement as another opportunity to connect with the reader. Your objective statement should be nothing more than the *exact* title of the job for which you are applying.

Do not use a general statement that describes how you want to work for a progressive, innovative and forward-thinking group practice or hospital. After all, aren't all medical groups and hospitals forward-thinking, progressive and innovative, at least in the eyes of those who will review your resume?

Here's are examples of objective statements that don't connect with the reader; all they do is force the reader to struggle through one or two seconds of excess reading:

Objective Statement

Management position with an progressive, expanding, innovative group practice to successfully achieve operating goals on a cost-effective basis.

or

Objective Statement

To be successful in a senior executive management position with a progressively governed health care organization that will support competent, productive and innovative leadership.

Ask yourself, "If I were screening either of these resumes and read these objective statements, what do they tell me about the candidate?" "Does this person have the background to do the job?" Your response: Neither statement tells me anything about the candidate. And you waste part of the 15 seconds.

Review this next client's example.

Objective Statement

I am looking for a job that will give me experience in the professional world while I take time off school.

Keep in mind, here's an objective statement that appears at the top of a resume – one of the first things a reviewer sees. What's your reaction to this statement? Yes, it's an honest statement; this client at the time was taking time between degree programs. But, what message does it send? The first message is, "I'm inexperienced" and the second message is "I won't work for too long because I'm going back to school." Not a positive way to begin your resume. Not many reviewers would read further. The result: the screen-out pile.

Now if you were responding to a classified ad in the *MGM Update* that was titled Managed Care Director, then your objective statement would be:

Objective Statement

Managed Care Director.

That's it; that's what you say. If the classified ad indicated the type or the size of the group practice or hospital, then you could add that piece of information. For example, if the ad described the facility as a newly integrated health care system looking for an individual with experience in a managed care setting, your objective statement could read:

Objective Statement

Director of managed care in a newly integrated health care system.

Or if the ad indicated a need for a Director of Managed Care for a Ophthalmology group, your objective statement would read:

Objective Statement

Director of managed care for an ophthalmology group.

This may seem silly to merely restate the obvious to the reader, but it's not. I've had several clients who, when called for a second or third interview, have asked how their resume was selected for the first round in interviews. The response – was that "your job objective is the same as the job we have open." The connection was made. Remember your objective. You should be able to state it very succinctly by now. Yes, that's correct, your only objective is to get a face-to-face interview with that organization and help the screener make that decision in 15 seconds or less. A specifically targeted objective statement will help you accomplish that goal.

One last note on objective statements. When you need to provide someone with an overview of your background and experience, and you're NOT applying for a specific job, then do one of two things. Either omit it altogether or use a clear and succinct statement that describes your career goal. Here's an example:

Objective Statement

Chief administrative director in a newly integrated health care system.

Continuing to build an example of a chronological resume:

Janet Smith
1111 South Jackson Street
Denver, CO 80012
(303) 555 - 1212 (Home)
(303) 555 - 1213 (Fax)

Objective Statement

Director of managed care in a newly integrated health care system.

Professional summary or qualifications statement

Your professional summary is a short and concise statement that summarizes your professional history and your qualifications. The purpose of using a summary statement is to provide readers with a snapshot of your professional history (qualifications) that captures their attention. Here are four examples:

Example 1: Someone with seven years of administrative experience.

A certified medical practice executive with extensive expertise in financial planning and analysis; operations management; strategic and business planning; third-party reimbursement; collections; account receivable; human resource management and new business development.

Example 2: A clinic manager with more than 20 years of group administrative experience:

Extensive career in hospital and clinic administration, with steady progression to higher levels of management positions each with increased span of authority, responsibility and accountability. As manager in two positions in clinic administration, provided leadership in managed care contracting, negotiating capitated plans, computerization, staffing, billing systems and facility expansion.

Example 3: A physician executive who moved from the clinic to administration:

Physician executive with extensive clinical experience and five years in medical management. Demonstrated strengths in organization, utilization review, quality assurance programs, strategic planning, financial planning, practice acquisition, physician recruitment, inpatient case management consultation, and managed care environment.

NOTES

Example 4: A college student recently graduated with an MHA degree and looking for a first full-time job in health care administration:

Completed an administrative fellowship at Riverwood University Medical Center working closely with the Associate Chief Operating Officer and rotating through all hospital and medical center departments. Provided consultative and administrative support to the Vice President of Corporate Services at Riverwood. Worked on projects involved in strategic planning, financial management, reviewing managed care contracts, and total quality management.

As you review each of these statements, think how you could customize each one for different situations. Each example includes a list of experiences and qualifications which could be re-ordered based on the specific needs and requirements of the organization. Place those that are of greater interest earlier in the sequence.

Do you have a professional summary statement? Should it be revised?

How do I find this information?

You may be wondering how to find this information if you haven't talked with someone from the organization. If you have a classified ad, those needs are usually listed as critical job requirements, experiences required, or qualifications. The most important requirements are usually listed first. Your job is to choose the important information contained in each classified ad.

Review the following classified ad. Pick out the key facts. Then, review the first two professional summaries presented above. Think how you might revise either summary based on the information (needs) presented in the ad.

Chief Executive Officer

Multi-speciality group practice with 25 physicians is searching for an experienced health care executive to provide overall administrative leadership to this growing organization. Strong skills and experience in strategic planning, financial management, managed care,and group operations a must.

Qualifications include a master's degree in business or health care administration with 7+ years executive level experience, 5+ years in group administration.

Mail resume and salary history to: (Contact name, address and phone number provided.)

What are the important clues presented in the ad? How would you revise the professional summary but still use the same information? As you select the key points, you are making assumptions about the needs of the organization. You could focus on these need areas:

1. *Senior level position.* I would add a number to the summary statement for years of experience. For example: Over 12 years of executive level experience including six years in group-practice administration.

2. *Size of the group.* A key piece of information is that the ad lists 25 physicians. Provide detail regarding work experience in larger physician groups.

3. *Growing organization.* This statement is mentioned early in the ad so you should assume growth is a major need. The question becomes, how could you edit your summary statement to reflect your experience at growing or expanding a group practice?

4. *List of experiences required.* Note that the list of skills is given in a specific order with strategic planning first. You should list strategic planning first in your statement and then add the others.

Here's how our resume looks so far:

Janet Smith
1111 South Jackson Street
Denver, CO 80012
(303) 555 - 1212 (Home)
(303) 555 - 1213 (Fax)

Objective Statement

Director of managed care in a newly integrated health care system.

Professional Summary

More than 12 years of executive-level experience including six years in group-practice administration with steady progression to higher levels of management positions, each with increased span of authority, responsibility and accountability. As manager in two positions in clinic administration, led strategic planning, contracting for managed care, negotiating capitated plans, computerizing records, staffing, improving billing systems, and expanding offices and equipment.

A final thought before moving on to the next section. You can also call the professional summary section "Qualifications" and include a listing of qualifications that closely matches the position requirements. Here's an example of how it might look:

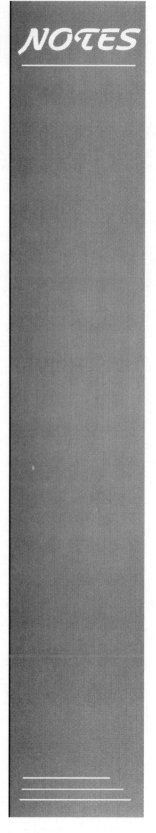

Janet Smith
1111 South Jackson Street
Denver, CO 80012
(303) 555 - 1212 (Home)
(303) 555 - 1213 (Fax)

Objective Statement

Director of acquisitions and mergers in a newly integrated health care system.

Qualifications

- Identified physician practices as merger/ acquisition candidates.
- Performed market research demographic research.
- Conducted merger/acquisition negotiations.
- Reviewed all merger/acquisition accounting and operations due diligence and pro forma development.
- Handled all post merger/acquisition transitions.

You can then expand on the qualification statement by describing them as detailed accomplishment statements in the body of your resume.
Selecting qualifications that match the requirements of the position will greatly increase your
chances of surviving the initial screening.

Professional experience

In this section, present details of your work experience including names of group practices and
organizations you've worked for, their locations,
your job titles, employment dates, and most
important, statements that describe examples of
your past accomplishments and achievements.
These are summary descriptions, including
results or outcomes of your work, of projects,
assignments, tasks, activities that you've completed – your accomplishments.

This information is the backbone of your resume;
it's what demonstrates your value, versatility and
volition.

Notice how the professional experience is presented in the continuing Janet Smith example:

Janet Smith
1111 South Jackson Street
Denver, CO 80012
(303) 555 - 1212 (Home)
(303) 555 - 1213 (Fax)

Objective Statement

Director of managed care in a newly integrated health care system.

Professional Summary

More than 12 years of executive-level experience including six years in group-practice administration with steady progression to higher levels of management positions, each with increased span of authority, responsibility and accountability. As manager in two positions in clinic administration, led strategic planning, contracting for managed care, negotiating capitated plans, computerizing records, staffing, improving billing systems, and expanding offices and equipment.

Professional Experience

Midwest Physicians Group   **1990 - Present**
Administrator

Senior executive responsible for the daily operations of a 35-physician multi-specialty group practice with three primary-care satellite clinics, 250 employees, and gross billings of $35 million. Directed the activities of all administrative and support functions.

- Proposed and completed a three-year project that added 13,000 square feet and renovated 18,000 square feet into a state-of-the-art facility.

- Recruited ten physicians in five years. Recruitment was based on patient availability and a strategic master plan that increased medical services within a pre-determined service area.

- Evaluated three computer billing, accounting and management reporting systems; recommended replacement system to improve communications for patient billing and collections.

- Created a system to schedule and track patients through follow-up and evaluations – an essential process whenever referrals are made under managed care.

- Prepared the first operations and capital budget for a hospital with $35 million   in revenues; it became standard part of financial reporting.

- Administered a pension and profit-sharing plan for 60 employees. Monitored the plan; handled contract changes including funding, dependency and distribution. Developed contracts with legal counsel, financial advisors and banks.

- Designed a program to train and use people across departments; reduced payments to temporary employment agencies by 75 percent.

- Negotiated salary contracts and, by eliminating overtime, reduced salary expenses by $500,000 the first year.

- Created a just-in-time inventory. By controlling use, standardizing and training, reduced expenses for medical materials and drugs by $1.6 million while patient visits increased 15 percent.

Riverbend Clinic   **1985-1990**
Assistant Administrator

Managed a group of 15 family-practice physicians, including billing and collections, data processing, managed-care contracting, clinic maintenance and financial management. Managed 54 staff.

- Created and administered a program to manage workers' compensation,establishing case management with a computerized tracking system that coordinated care and improved communication with employers and insurers.

- Improved revenue collection by 35 percent for one year.

- Evaluated requirements for outpatients, related options, and costs – accurately compared vendors and provided information for long-term decisions.

This example demonstrates several important aspects of the chronological resume:

1. Notice how each organization and your job title are identified and positioned. The example has the organization listed first, followed by the job title underneath. This can be switched, listing your job title first, followed by the organization. It's your decision if you want to focus the reader on your organization or title.

2. The next piece of information is a short one-or-two sentence summary describing the organization and your major responsibilities. This quickly lets the reader know a little bit about the organization you are (or were) with as well as the scope of your responsibilities. It's also another opportunity to connect with the reader by indicating how your experience matches their requirements.

3. Note the use of accomplishment statements; – how each is written in short-story format. Also notice the use of numbers either in percentages, dollars or size. Readers will remember numbers. Numbers demonstrate your uniqueness. Use them whenever possible. Also notice how outcomes or results are mentioned in some of the statements. Remember those two questions I talked about earlier:

    •   What did you do when you did that?
    •   So what?

Answering the "So what?" question will help you identify outcomes/results. Reference the section in this chapter for a detailed review on writing accomplishing statements.

Let's continue by describing the last two sections of a chronological resume: 1) education; and 2) related professional information.

Education and related professional information

In this section list degrees, licenses or certificates attained. List your academic degrees first beginning with your highest or most recent. Certifications and licenses follow. It's also important to list any and all certificates in this section. If you achieved the Certified Healthcare Executive certification, list it here. If you are a nominee for the American College of Medical Practice Executives, list that in this section.

Review the following examples and then see how they fit into our continuing Janet Smith example:

Education

Master of Science in Health Administration; University of Colorado Health Sciences; 1985.

Bachelor of Science, Business Administration; University of Colorado at Boulder; 1980.

Fellow, American College of Medical Practice Executives (ACMPE); 1990

The last section of a chronological resume is a listing of any related professional information that doesn't fit anywhere else in the resume but is still important. This includes memberships, affiliations and any other information that is directly related to the job or position you are applying for. Refer to the following example:

Related Professional Information

Kansas Medical Group Management Association
    Chapter President: 1992 - 1993

Midland County Chamber of Commerce
    Completed Leadership class - 1989

Clinical Laboratory Management Association
    Member since 1992

Medical Group Management Association: National
Member since 1985

Healthcare Financial Management Association
Member since 1993

Don't include personal information such as family members' names, health, hobbies, etc. Although important to you, they don't add value to your resume. This information usually comes out during your interviews.

Some "borderline" information, such as leadership experience in service organizations, may be relevant. I recommend you include it in your resume database. Then decide whether to use it whenever you prepare a customized resume for each job opportunity.

References

Just a note on including references in your resume – don't. We all have references – good references. You don't need to take space on a resume to say "References provided on request." Employers assume you'll provide them when asked.

Now, here's a sample chronological resume that a client customized for the position of Director of Managed Care in a newly integrated health care system.

Janet Smith
1111 South Jackson Street
Denver, CO 80012
(303) 555 - 1212 (Home)
(303) 555 - 1213 (Fax)

Objective Statement

Director of managed care in a newly integrated health care system.

Professional Summary

More than 12 years of executive-level experience including six years in group-practice administration with steady progression to higher levels of management positions, each with increased span of authority, responsibility and accountability. As manager in two positions in clinic administration, led strategic planning, contracting for managed care, negotiating capitated plans, computerizing records, staffing, improving billing systems, and expanding offices and equipment.

Professional Experience

Midwest Physicians Group   **1990 - Present**
Administrator

Senior executive responsible for the daily operations of a 35-physician multi-specialty group practice with three primary-care satellite clinics, 250 employees, and gross billings of $35 million. Directed the activities of all administrative and support functions.

- Proposed and completed a three-year project that added 13,000 square feet and renovated 18,000 square feet into a state-of-the-art facility.

- Recruited ten physicians in five years. Recruitment was based on patient availability and a strategic master plan that increased medical services within a pre-determined service area.

- Evaluated three computer billing, accounting and management reporting systems; recommended replacement system to improve communications for patient billing and collections.

- Created a system to schedule and track patients through follow-up and evaluations – an essential process whenever referrals are made under managed care.

- Prepared the first operations and capital budget for a hospital with $35 million in revenues; it became standard part of financial reporting.

- Administered a pension and profit-sharing plan for 60 employees. Monitored the plan; handled contract changes including funding, dependency and distribution. Developed contracts with legal counsel, financial advisors and banks.

- Designed a program to train and use people across departments; reduced payments to temporary employment agencies by 75 percent.

- Negotiated salary contracts and, by eliminating overtime, reduced salary expense by $500,000 the first year.

- Created a just-in-time inventory. By controlling use, standardizing, and training, reduced expenses for medical materials and drugs by $1.6 million while patient visits increased 15 percent.

Riverbend Clinic   **1985 -1990**
Assistant Administrator

Managed a group of 15 family-practice physicians, including billing and collections, data processing, managed-care contracting, clinic maintenance and financial management. Managed 54 staff.

- Created and administered a program to manage workers' compensation, establishing case management with a computerized tracking system that coordinated care and improved communication with employers and insurers.

- Improved revenue collection by 35 percent for one year.

- Evaluated requirements for outpatients, related options and costs – accurately compared vendors and provided information for long-term decisions.

- Designed a customer satisfaction reporting system that responded to patient and family concerns within 24 hours of the complaint. This became part of the patient quality assurance program.

Education

Master of Science in Health Administration; University of Colorado Health Sciences; 1985.

Bachelor of Science, Business Administration; University of Colorado at Boulder; 1980.

Fellow, American College of Medical Practice Executives (ACMPE); 1990

Related Professional Information

Kansas Medical Group Management Association
   Chapter President: 1992 - 1993

Midland County Chamber of Commerce
   Completed Leadership class - 1989

Clinical Laboratory Management Association
   Member since 1992

Medical Group Management Association: National
   Member since 1985

Healthcare Financial Management Association
   Member since 1993

Using a functional format

The functional format organizes your work experience by functional area, the things you did, not by when or where you did them. This format is often useful when you're changing careers or professions. It includes the same key information (accomplishments); it's just presented differently. The chronological format emphasizes your employment history ordered by time; the functional format allows you to highlight your experience and accomplishments in areas such as Administration, Finance, Management, Human Resources, Integration and Strategic Planning.

This format has its critics who suggest you're using it only to hide some aspect of your work history. I don't buy that argument. This format presents your background in a way that can capture the reader's attention faster. Remember, your goal is to connect with readers. They don't immediately think, "Ah ha! I wonder what this person is trying to hide? I better skip this one," when they see a resume using a functional format. In fact, you may connect better if your research uncovers four or five functional areas of critical interest to the organization. For example, you may find out that Administration, Facilities, Customer Service, and Budget/Finance are critical areas for an organization hiring a practice manager or hospital administrator. Doesn't it make sense to organize your accomplishments under these functional headings? You can still list your employment history later in the resume. You're not hiding anything; you're simply making it easier for readers to quickly understand your potential value to their organizations.

When will a functional format work best?

A functional format may be appropriate whenever you:

• Are changing careers and it's critical how the skills and experience from your current job or profession transfer to another. For example, administrators with 14 years of experience who use a chronological format may have difficulty getting interviews with organizations in education or telecommunications. Why? Because the format focuses a reader on their health care experience and not on skills that would transfer – managing, finance, budgeting, negotiating and contracting. The reader's immediate reaction would be, "This person doesn't have experience or education in telecommunications." But the candidate may have the "exact" required skills that are easily transferred.

• Want to emphasize skills not in your most recent work experience. This is also important when changing careers or when you decide you want to "get back into the job I loved the most."

• Are entering the job market for the first time. Most undergraduate and graduate students should use functional resumes. This allows them to highlight the skills used and learned throughout school from internships, school projects or assignments that aren't jobs. These skills are very difficult to capture in chronological order.

• Have various different and unconnected experiences. Here's the situation in which some people feel you'd be "hiding" an experience gap or some kind of "undesirable" history. However, there may be hundreds of reasons for having a break in employment, none of which should automatically screen you out of consideration for a position. Today's professional may: 1) take time to be at home with small children while the other spouse is the main breadwinner; 2) take an extended absence to care for elderly parents; or 3) take time to complete another degree or certificate program. Someone may decide to meet a strong personal need by enrolling in the Peace Corps for one or two years. All create a break in service in the traditional sense; none is a legitimate reason to screen you out.

How do I create a functional resume?

For the functional format, the heading, objective statement and professional summary are identical to those in the chronological format. But you cover accomplishments in functional groups, such as:

- Administration and organization
- Finance
- Budgeting and accounting
- Human resources
- Customer service
- Facilities management
- Construction

You then follow this section with your professional history, listing each group practice, hospital or organization where you've worked, usually on the second or third page of a resume. You can see why this format is great for people changing careers. Readers immediately review and react to accomplishments that meet their needs, not to your lack of industry experience. By the time readers get to the section on organizations, they may have already decided you're a match and schedule an interview. At least you are giving yourself a fighting chance to have this happen; they aren't immediately screening you out.

Look at the next page to review a sample functional resume using the same Janet Smith example.

Janet Smith
1111 South Jackson Street
Denver, CO 80012
(303) 555 - 1212 (Home)
(303) 555 - 1213 (Fax)

Objective Statement

Director of managed care in a newly integrated health care system.

Professional Summary

More than 12 years of executive-level experience including six years in group-practice administration with steady progression to higher levels of management positions, each with increased span of authority, responsibility and accountability. As manager in two positions in clinic administration, led strategic planning, contracting for managed care, negotiating capitated plans, computerizing records, staffing, improving billing systems, and expanding offices and equipment.

Professional Experience

Finance and Budget

- Administered a pension and profit-sharing plan for 60 employees. Monitored the plan; handled contract changes including funding, dependency and distribution. Developed contracts with legal counsel, financial advisors and banks.

- Created and administered a program to manage workers' compensation, establishing case management with a computerized tracking system that coordinated care and improved communication with employers and insurers.

- Prepared the first operations and capital budget for a hospital with $35 million in revenues; it became part of standard financial reporting.

- Improved revenue collection by 35 percent for one year.

- Created a just-in-time inventory. By controlling use, standardizing, and training, reduced expenses for medical materials and drugs by $1.6 million while patient visits increased 15 percent.

Administration and Organization

- Recruited ten physicians in five years. Recruitment was based on patient availability and a strategic master plan that increased medical services within a pre-determined service area.

- Evaluated three computer billing, accounting and management reporting systems; recommended replacement system to improve communications for patient billing and collections.

- Proposed and completed a three-year project that added 13,000 square feet and renovated 18,000 square feet into a state-of-the-art facility.

- Created a system to schedule and track patients through follow-up and evaluations – an essential process whenever referrals are made under managed care.

- Designed a program to train and use people across departments; reduced payments to temporary employment agencies by 75 percent.

- Negotiated salary contracts and, by eliminating overtime, reduced salary expenses by $500,000 the first year.

Customer Service

- Evaluated requirements for outpatients, related option, and costs – accurately compared vendors and provided information for long-term decisions.

- Designed a customer satisfaction reporting system that responded to patient and family concerns within 24 hours of the complaint. This became part of the patient quality assurance program.

Professional History

Midwest Physicians Group;   **1990 - Present**
Midway, KS 11111
Administrator

Senior executive responsible for the daily operations of a 35-physician multi-specialty group practice with three primary-care satellite clinics, 250 employees, and gross billings of $35 million. Directed the activities of all administrative and support functions.

Riverbend Clinic;   **1985 - 1990**
Midway, KS 11111
Assistant Administrator

Managed a group of 15 family-practice physicians, including billing and collections, data processing, managed-care contracting, clinic maintenance and financial management. Managed 54 staff.

Education

Master of Science in Health Administration; University of Colorado Health Sciences; 1985.

Bachelor of Science, Business Administration; University of Colorado at Boulder; 1980.

Fellow, American College of Medical Practice Executives (ACMPE); 1990

Related Professional Information

Kansas Medical Group Management Association
> Chapter President: 1992 - 1993

Midland County Chamber of Commerce
> Completed Leadership class - 1989

Clinical Laboratory Management Association
> Member since 1992

Medical Group Management Association: National
> Member since 1985

Health care Financial Management Association
> Member since 1993

Notice how this format helps readers focus on the functional areas your accomplishments and experience relate to, not on the organizations you've worked with. Once readers see that your experience and background match their needs, they focus less on the fact that your experience is in a different industry. You're persuading readers to look more deeply at what you can do, rather than glancing at where you've worked and screening you out.

Look at your resume. Which format are you using? How would you benefit from using another format?

Marketing letters

Let's look at a third type of "resume" – the marketing letter. Effective marketing letters may help you schedule face-to-face meetings more easily than a traditional resume.

Gaining the attention of a busy executive, board chairman, physician or hiring manager is difficult. Marketing letters bring a breath of fresh air to your job search and may get you past an ever-alert executive secretary looking to intercept traditional resumes and cast them (like demons) into the personnel files. They may help you avoid the boilerplate memo from human resources saying, "There are no openings, but we'll keep your resume on file for six months."

Marketing letters succeed for four reasons: 1) they are a more personal approach; 2) very few people use them; 3) they might get face-to-face appointments when an opening doesn't exist; and 4) they are a way to expand your network list. A marketing letter is an expanded cover letter that emphasizes skills and achievements directly related to the organization's needs.

Here's an example:

June 12, 1998

Dr. Albert Jones
Southwest Medical Group
1111 West Drive
Dallas, TX 12345

Dear Dr. Jones:

At Janet Smith's urging, I'm forwarding some information about myself for your consideration. After careful thought, I've recognized the integration you are now going through, plus your need to maintain patients' satisfaction, may require some senior experience and additional leadership.

My thinking stems from my recent experience managing a similar integration for which I:

- Developed consolidated budgets for medical and non-medical capital expenses to build a new 35,000-square foot wing.

- Evaluated requirements for an outpatient computer system. Studied alternatives for integrating two existing systems versus designing a new one.

- Developed medical-staffing plans for primary-care and subspecialty clinics while coordinating with the medical directors and boards from both organizations. The plans included designing and locating two satellite practices for primary care.

I will call next Thursday at 3:00 pm to arrange a convenient time to discuss these experiences with you.

Sincerely;

John McDonald
Vice President
(303) 555 - 1212

In this example, the three bullets directly match the reader's requirements or needs so it may connect "emotionally" with him. Struggling with the problems integration creates, he might welcome talking with someone who has been through (and survived) the experience.

A marketing letter contains three important sections:

1. An introduction that invites the person to keep reading.

2. Three or four accomplishment statements directly related to the needs or environment of the person or organization.

3. Your closing which states the action you will take or next steps.

Review the sample letter again. Is the introduction "stimulating" enough to make the person want to continue reading? How would you revise it? Are the accomplishment statements clear and descriptive? Pay close attention to the closing sentence. Does it sound too pushy or forward? Some clients like this kind of approach; others think it's too strong. It all depends on your style and preference. Personally, I like it. And I have many clients who report that hiring managers liked this approach.

At first, some of my clients wonder whether the marketing letter makes sense, especially if they don't include their career history. But because this approach isn't used much, I believe it creates a certain mystery for the executive who receives it. Administrators and other executives I've spoken to said they would be inclined to talk to the person for two reasons:

1. The author hit on a current and specific need; and

2. They like how the person took the initiative and believe they would like this type of person working for them.

130

Remember, the marketing letter has two goals: 1) To get an interview if a job opening exists; and 2) to get a face-to-face meeting when an opening doesn't exist but you'd like to find out more about that organization. You may help the executive identify a specific need and create a position for yourself.

Marketing letters work! Employers are impressed with candidates who take the time and have the imagination and creativity to develop leads and contacts using this approach. These letters can get face-to-face interviews.

Here's what I hope you remember about resumes and marketing letters

1. Length is NOT an issue. Yes, every reference you read will advise, "Keep your resume to one or two pages." That's good advice except for one small problem. It's impossible for people with more than two or three years of experience to condense it into one or two pages and still hope to connect with the reader's needs. You may get "lucky" and just happen to match those needs. But the reader's response is more likely to be, "Oh well, just another typical resume. I'll keep looking through the pile and maybe come back to this one." Chances are your resume won't be looked at again.

2. Powerful arrangement – to capture attention and meet needs within 15 seconds – is an issue. Be sure you know enough about the organization you're applying to so you can confidently match your experience and background to the reader's needs and interests in the first 1-1/2 pages of your resume. The first page of your resume is your cover letter. In the earlier Janet Smith example, this means readers will have screened in or out by the time they read to about the third or fourth bullet under the Midwest Physicians group (including cover letter).

NOTES

131

3. You must customize each cover letter and resume. Don't merely bundle up and mail your "one-size-fits-all" resume along with a generic cover letter. Your job is to research the position and organization to learn enough to customize your material to the needs of that organization. If you do, readers will choose to read past page two; they will be interested and want to read further. You won't know this has happened, but when it does, your resume will have accomplished its only purpose – to get the attention of readers so they'll call you for an interview.

I know this process works because I consistently hear stories from clients who have been sending resumes for three or four months with little or no response – not even the generic response that "we received your resume and will keep it on file for six months." Translation – we pitched it; don't call us again. Clients are confused about not getting a response. They believe they have excellent experience that seems to match the job perfectly, based on information in the classified ad. And it probably is a good match. But their cover letters and resumes just don't capture the reader's attention. They don't motivate the reader to pick up the phone to call for an interview.

In each situation, the person was using a one-size-fits-all resume. People screening the resumes didn't quickly identify a match. Nothing in the material sparked interest. Once my clients learned how to customize cover letters and resumes to each situation, the phone started ringing. In one case, a client on the East Coast hadn't received **one** response from over 50 mailings to specific classified ads. Once we talked about how to research each opportunity and customize the cover letter and resume, follow-up calls began within two weeks.

4. A functional resume format is as effective as a chronological one. Analyze each situation before you determine which format to use. Consider situations in which you could use a marketing letter. Fit the format to your needs.

5. Be sure your objective statement is nothing more than the job title of the position you're applying for. Keep it short and direct. Omit the objective statement if you're using the resume with a contact person and not for a specific position.

Change in the health care market is creating a different job-search environment. If you're searching today, you can't merely send resumes to 10 classified ads and expect four or five interviews; too many applicants make it an "employers' market." You must make your resume stand out, not by using colored paper or fancy fonts or photos, but by connecting with readers based on how your background matches their needs.

Next we'll discuss the key ingredients of your resume – accomplishment statements.

Accomplishments or result statements: Your resume's key ingredient

Employers are looking for someone who can solve problems, make decisions that affect the bottom line, and the help the organization reach its goals. In other words, employers have needs. It's your job, as a candidate for a position, to match your skills, abilities and experience – your accomplishments and achievements – to those needs. You must persuade or convince people you can help them meet their needs – and at first you must do so in writing, not in person.

Preparing accomplishment statements that accurately represent and describe your background is THE critical first step in your job search and in developing your resume database. Here's why. Of

133

course, the goal of your job search is to find the ideal position that matches your values, skills, interests and environmental requirements. To find that new job, you must receive an offer. To receive an offer, you must interview. To interview, you must use a customized resume and cover letter. To develop customized resumes and cover letters it's useful to have a resume database. To develop a resume database you must write accomplishment or achievement statements. The process looks like this:

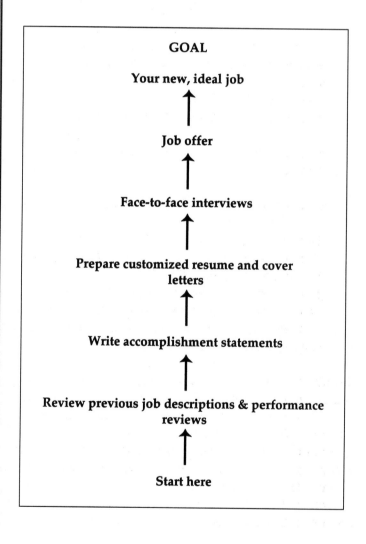

How do I write accomplishment statements?

In this section, I'll discuss writing accomplishment statements for resumes and cover letters. You'll use a slightly different approach for resumes that are electronically scanned or prepared for the Internet. I'll discuss those later.

Accomplishment statements are:

- More than a restated job description or summary of past responsibilities.

- Descriptions of specific professional and personal experiences. They describe completed projects, assignments and tasks; cross-functional teams you've led or participated in; and outcomes of your work or volunteer experiences.

- Specific examples of your skills, abilities and knowledge.

- Clues about your talents and qualifications.

- Short paragraphs that describe your "value" to someone who is interested in hiring you. The more you can describe how your background and experiences match the needs of prospective employers, the greater your value to them and the greater your chances that they will call you for an interview.

Think of accomplishment statements as short, descriptive stories: two or three concise sentences that describe what you did for a task, activity or project. Describe a result or outcome. Your goal is to create a picture in the reader's mind about what you did in each situation, the results and their effect on the organization. To do this well, make sure each accomplishment statement includes three parts:

1. The action you took. Begin each statement with an action verb that describes what you did.

NOTES

135

2. The outcome or result of your action. Be sure to include a quantitative measure or number such as dollars saved, customers increased, or revenue generated, etc.

3. The scope of your work. This describes the project or task.

When developing accomplishment statements, think of situations where you have:

- Improved administrative procedures and processes, office work flow, accounting or bookkeeping functions, or work efficiency.

- Reduced costs and expenses, turnover, administrative processing time, or amounts of accounts receivable.

- Developed new procedures, programs, processes or manuals for handling an activity more efficiently.

- Initiated change, new policies or creative programs that improved the practice's performance.

Whenever possible, use numbers – percentages, revenue generated, decreased expenses, etc. Numbers command the reader's attention and help to highlight your past accomplishments.

An example

I introduced two questions in my discussion on the resume database:

1) *What did I do when I did that?*

and,

2) *So what?*

Use these questions to develop unique accomplishment statements. I'll use managed-care contracting as the sample situation. Let's say one of your current responsibilities is to negotiate managed-care contracts for your medical group. Thinking about your responsibility, you might write the following accomplishment statement:

Researched and negotiated the first managed-care contracts for the group.

I've seen many resumes with this same accomplishment statement. Now, put yourself in the shoes of an employer. What does this statement say, really? Not much. How does this statement help you to stand out from the other 25 or 30 resumes that employer might be reviewing? It doesn't! How many other group-practice administrators have experience negotiating managed-care contracts? Probably most of them. Does this statement demonstrate uniqueness? No. Would it make you stand out? No.

To develop a personalized "story" describing your experience in negotiating managed-care contracts, ask yourself the first question – "What did I do when I negotiated these contracts?" Expand your thinking by brainstorming every task or activity you did when you negotiated contracts.

Ask yourself, "When I was involved in negotiating our first managed-care contract, what did I do?" Following are examples of your possible activities:

1. Clarified the needs of the group practice and the needs of the physicians. I identified what the physicians wanted to accomplish.

2. Researched which third-party payers were looking at establishing contracts in our market area and interviewed all potential third-party payers.

3. Analyzed the contracts; prepared a report outlining how each would affect our group.

4. Provided recommendations, actions and plans for the physicians to discuss; analyzed different scenarios.

5.   Reviewed alternatives and scenarios with the physicians; responded to their questions and concerns.

6.   Carried out physicians' decisions; negotiated the contracts.

Now, think about the results of your work. Typical results might be:

1.   Increased our share in one particular market segment by 35 percent during the first year of the contract.

2.   Clarified physicians' expectations and objectives.

From these results, you could write a more comprehensive accomplishment statement:

Increased patient load 35 percent in one year by establishing the first managed-care contracts for the practice. Researched and negotiated with the HMO; made sure physician objectives were written into the contract; set up new administrative systems that support the new contracts; trained office staff; monitored the process monthly.

Here's another example of a detailed accomplishment statement that tells your story:

Increased clinic revenues 25 percent and physicians' yearly compensation 15 percent each year for the last four years by enhancing revenue and reducing expenses:

- *Recovered $1.2 million in initially denied, unpaid, insurance claims.*

- *Established four federally certified rural health clinics and increased revenues more than $500,000 per year; increased medical access for Medicare and Medicaid patients in the community.*

- *Analyzed the group's coding process and modified it to correct undercharging. I anticipate this new program will increase revenues by 17 percent each year.*

- *Negotiated favorable contracts with managed-care companies.*

In this example, four different actions (accomplishments) help to describe, in detail, your accomplishment – increasing clinic revenues 25 percent and physician compensation 15 percent in each of the last four years. That statement will capture the reader's attention. Continue by describing how you increased revenues and physicians' compensation. Notice that in this example the statement describing managed-care contracts can stand alone, whereas in the example, when it was used as a main theme, it was more effective to explain in detail.

Following are other sample accomplishment statements. Notice the action verbs, results and outcomes, and the scope (description) of each activity. As you read these, pretend you're the employer reviewing the information for the first time. Do the statements paint a picture for you? What "value" would this person bring to your practice? How "versatile" is this person? What are some of the strong points that come to mind? Weak points? How do the figures and outcomes capture your attention? What other information would you like to know about this person that would make you want to schedule an interview?

1. *Coordinated activities and successfully completed a $2.6 million, 35,000-square-foot addition to the building which added 50 percent more revenue-generating floor space. Completed the addition without disruption to patient services and flow.*

2. *Established an ambulatory surgery center for the group.*

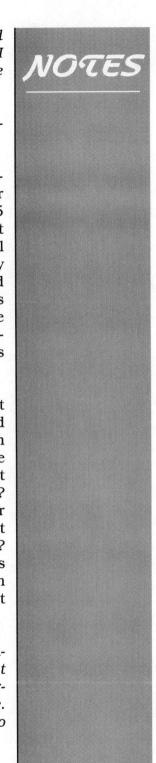

NOTES

NOTES

3. Improved our public image by designing and carrying out a successful marketing campaign that consists of a balanced use of newspaper and radio ads, community-service projects and an Internet web site.

4. Obtained, reviewed and negotiated provider contracts for the surgery center and multi-physician practice with MCOs, including Part A and Part B Medicare dollars.

5. Increased net income $400,000 in the first year by developing a program to analyze RBRVS coding and restructuring the fee schedule. Anticipate a $250,000 increase in net income increase over the next three years.

6. Researched and created a program for incentive compensation to physicians; increased production more than $1,000,000 annually in an environment of declining physician revenues.

7. Researched and analyzed a major program to convert computers to new software for the clinic and three satellite offices. Coordinated to complete the conversion in one-half the budgeted time and $25,000 under budget. Planned and led internal training for all staff and physicians.

8. Expanded from 88 to 117 multi-specialty medical staff members while reducing staffing from 6.1:1 to 4.1:1 during the growth period.

9. Reduced overhead expenses to 42 percent of revenues, down from 59 percent over one year. Contributed to physician-shareholders' income.

10. Increased aggregate revenues collected by 25 percent; reduced average days in receivables from 129 days to 75 days; and increased the net collections from 87 percent to 96 percent.

11. *Provided foundation for a corporate restructuring and reorganization by rewriting the Amended and Restated Bylaws, which the professional corporation's shareholders approved and adopted.*

As you write accomplishment statements, think about:

•   Any previous experiences, projects or assignments that stood out for you – that you did well and enjoyed.

•   Activities you've been involved in that are unique – that you are good at that may have "value" to others,

•   Problems which you defined and solved.

Accomplishment statements are usually written in the past tense – researched, developed, etc. But sometimes, you may want to describe a project you are working on; it's something you're doing now. Use action statements like *"Developing a procedure to . . . ."* or *"Exploring new techniques for developing customer-service strategies . . . ."*

Your turn to write accomplishment statements

It's your turn – either revise your current resume or begin with your first draft. For those of you who already have a resume:

•   Review it.   I suspect you've combined accomplishment and responsibilities. I also suspect you haven't included every task, assignment or project because you were trying to keep it to two pages. Expand it now.

You may find it motivating once you get into the swing of things. We don't often take time to think about what we've accomplished over the years. You may be surprised – you've accomplished a lot.

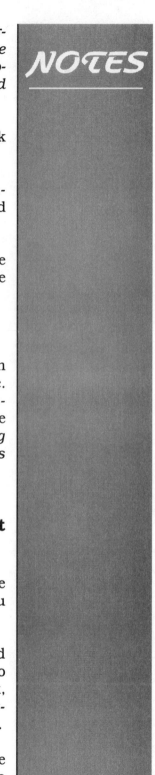

NOTES

To help you get started, I've provided:

1) Sample worksheet;
2) Lists of action verbs by functional category;
   - Leading and managing
   - Communication and communicating
   - Creating and innovating

3) List of headings used in functional resumes; and

4) Sample resumes, including one with accomplishment statements for a resume database.

Good luck and happy writing!

WORKSHEET
Writing Accomplishment Statements

Sample

My specific opportunity:

Find a way to decrease the time it takes to receive payment from all payers.   Goal: shorten cycle time for accounts payable.

Action(s) I took:

I researched, studied, analyzed, coordinated, designed, improved, sold an idea.

Results of my action for the company or people involved:

Payment rates increased during the next six months. Income cash flow improved for the group practice.

Accomplishment statement:

Increased payment rate by 75 percent on accounts receivable by creating a program for payment at time of service.

WORKSHEET

ACCOMPLISHMENT STATEMENTS

My specific opportunity:

Action(s) I took:

Results of my action for the company or people involved:

Accomplishment statement:

List of action verbs for your accomplishment statements

I've separated this list into categories that should help you identify appropriate verbs.

Leading and managing

administered	developed	inspected	reconciled
analyzed	discovered	led	recruited
assigned	delegated	marketed	resolved
achieved	diagnosed	maintained	retrieved
advised	eliminated	managed	reviewed
approved	established	mentored	reduced
appraised	estimated	met	researched
arranged	evaluated	modeled	saved
audited	examined	monitored	screened
balanced	forecasted	motivated	solved
budgeted	helped	negotiated	spearheaded
calculated	identified	obtained	specified
catalogued	improved	operated	streamlined
chaired	inspected	organized	supervised
classified	investigated	originated	surveyed
clarified	implemented	oversaw	systematized
collected	increased	piloted	trouble-shoot
completed	informed	projected	tabulated
compiled	initiated	planned	transformed
conducted	installed	prepared	uncovered
converted	instructed	purchased	word processed
decreased	introduced	prevented	
designed	investigated	provided	

Communicating

Adapted	convinced	facilitated	moderated
advised	corresponded	formulated	negotiated
addressed	consulted	guided	persuaded
arbitrated	counseled	informed	promoted
assisted	drafted	instructed	recruited
authored	diagnosed	interpreted	trained
clarified	edited	lectured	taught
coached	educated	mediated	performed
coordinated	explained	mentored	

Creating or innovating

assembled	founded	originated	repaired
calculated	illustrated	overhauled	shaped
computed	initiated	performed	solved
conceptualized	invented	planned	upgraded
created	innovated	programmed	wrote
customized	inspired	revitalized	
designed	identified	redesigned	
engineered	launched	remodeled	

Sample headings for your functional resume

These ideas for headings in a functional resume are here to help you think of others that might be appropriate in your situation.

Accounting	Fund Raising	Program
Acquisition	Goal Setting	Development
Administration	Graphic Design	Programming
Advertising/Marketing	Information Systems	Promotion
Advising	Innovation	Public Relations
Budget/Finance	Inspection	Public Speaking
Capitation	Instruction	Publicity
Coaching	Interviewing	Purchasing
Communications	Investigation	Quality Assurance/
Community Affairs	Investment Analysis	Quality Control
Conflict Resolution	Leadership	Real Estate
Construction	Legal Management	Research
Consulting	Management	Selling
Coordination	Assessment	Social Work
Counseling	Market Research	Special Events
Customer Service	Mathematics	Planning
Design	Motivation	Supervision
Drafting	Mentoring	Systems
Employment	Occupational Therapist	Teaching
Engineering	Optics	Technical Writing
Facilitation	Organization	Testing
Facilities	Organization Planning	Trouble Shooting
Finance	Presentations	Writing & Editing

Sample resumes

The following resumes represent various backgrounds and formats, along with my observations about each:

1) Resume database – shortened;

2) Person with a graduate degree looking for a first job in health care;

3) Director of nursing for a major community hospital; and

4) Chronological format customized to a position for a senior financial-operations manager.

Sample resume database with accomplishment stories: Shortened

Robert M. Jones
1234 Smith Street
Seattle, WA 99999
(206) 999 - 1234 (Home)
(206) 999 - 1111 (fax)

Qualifications

Experienced, results-oriented health care chief executive with a 22-year record of increasingly responsible positions and significant accomplishments in operating hospitals, medical group practices and related businesses. Major qualifications in operations, physician and hospital organizational relations, strategic planning, managed care contracts, and health system development.

Professional Experience

Maplewood Clinic, LTD.   **1995 - 1998**
Seattle, WA
Executive Manager & Chief Administrative Officer

*   Established an infrastructure for expansion including the creation of a Human Resources Department where no personnel function previously existed; a Marketing and Public Relations Department (the clinic had been without an organized marketing function for over three years); an Information Systems Department (none previously existed); a Finance Division headed by a Chief Financial Officer and Operations Division headed by a Chief Operating Officer formerly directed by an administrative director. Interviewed and hired senior management in each of these functions. Reduced corporate overhead expenses as a percentage of revenues by 25 percent while holding dollars spent constant at $6.5 million while hiring for these positions.

*   Developed and installed updated communications (e.g., voicemail, e-mail, and a web site) to:

    *   Augment the weekly physicians' meetings and written informational newsletter;
    *   Conducted monthly administrative staff breakfasts with employees; wrote a monthly administrative newsletter;

*   Daily visits to hospital to visit with surgeons' and daily "walk around" consultations throughout the clinic. Purpose of the walk around was to disseminate information and attempt to stay in touch with employees and physicians during a time of significant and rapid change.

•   Developed the framework of a physician practice management service organization equity corporation designed for the economic benefit of the physicians while positioning clinic as a market-driven organization that could take advantage of a possible purchase by others if the physician owners should decide to sell.

•   Selected and installed the +MEDIC Vision physician practice management system converting from a local service bureau billing service that had been in use for over 20 years. Demonstrated to the physicians how upgrading our system would save them money the first year of operation. Actually saved the clinic over $1.2 million dollars in the first year. Anticipate doubling that amount after the second year of operation. Trained all clinic staff on the system. Continue to monitor and respond to daily system problems; trouble-shoot solutions with staff.

NOTES

Note: This should be enough to give you an idea of how to write your "stories" that make up your resume database. They can be written in paragraph form listing your main activities for each accomplishment. Don't worry about length. Be sure to include a detailed description of your tasks and outcomes. When you customize, you can edit these stories into shorter accomplishment statements (one to three short sentences).

Your database should include information for each resume category:

• Heading;
• Objective statement;
• Professional summary statement;
• Professional experience listed in chronological order beginning with your most recent and moving backward until you've covered your entire work history;
• Education/certifications; and
• Related professional information.

Sample resume: Student with a graduate degree looking for a first job in health care

Susan Strong
4600 University Drive; Apt. 1001
Raleigh, NC 20000
(907) 555 - 1212

Professional Summary

Completed an Administrative Fellowship at Duke University Medical Center working closely with the Associate Chief Operating Officer and rotating through hospital and medical center departments. Provided consultative support to the Vice President of Corporate Services at Wildwood Health Care. Experience in planning, financial management, counseling and total quality management.

Professional Experience

Wildwood Health Care   **1996**
Durham, North Carolina
Intern Project Consultant

- Designed and implemented physician database used by the Health Plan Alliance for marketing patient services.

- Supported the hospital Outreach Laboratory Task Force:

  * Evaluated current pricing structure of all medical tests.
  * Created a graphic display of historical data used at several strategic planning retreats to establish goals and objectives.
  * Tabulated six months of test data for statistical analysis.

- Compiled and completed statistical information for North Carolina State Hospital License application.

Duke University Medical Center   **1994 - 1996**
Durham, North Carolina
Health Care Administrative Fellow

- Researched and wrote a plan on Adverse Food and Drug Reaction monitoring systems. Result: Plan was used hospital-wide and will help meet accreditation requirements.

- Served on the Continuous Quality Improvement Team to redesign and streamline Lined Distribution.

- Redesigned Gynecology/Oncology Business Plan format and updated tables, data and strategic goals.

- Developed improvements to the Surgical Waiting Area:

  * Created and administered needs assessment survey. Tabulated, analyzed and presented conclusions to Executive Committee. Result: All recommendations accepted and plans implemented.

- Participated on a team that developed and implemented the first medical center-wide orientation curriculum:

  * Established program objectives
  * Curriculum design
  * Trained managers on program content
  * Developed materials
  * Designed evaluation techniques

- Devised a Visiting Observer Policy for the Credentials Committee. New policy was used extensively throughout the hospital.

Smith Health Care Corporation   **1993 - 1994**
Johnstown, North Carolina
Administrative Resident

- Played an important role in preparing the corporation for accreditation by the Joint Commission on the Accreditation of Healthcare Organizations.

- Participated in the corporate strategic planning conference helping the organization set goals and objectives.

- Assisted in preparing grant applications.

- Developed and implemented a diabetes and hypertension protocol for utilization by the physicians and nursing staff.

- Organized, developed and implemented a tri-county corporation disaster plan and drill procedure.

Redstone Internal Medicine   **Fall 1992**
Albany, New York
Intern Project Consultant

- Created a business plan for the group practice.

- Collected financial, human resource, operations and demographic data on the practice to help create the business plan.

- Made the presentation and prepared the final report of the business plan to all group practice staff and board.

Albany Memorial Hospital   **Summer 1992**
Albany, New York
Intern Project Consultant

- Created a system for more complete and accurate tracking of physician expenses and diagnosis.

- Conducted feasibility study for establishment of hospice services within the hospital.

- Participated in senior team meetings and hospital rotations.

Knight Adult Day Care Services   **Spring 1992**
Newtown, New York
Needs Assessment Intern

- Wrote recommendations and presented results for future direction of the agency. Recommendations based upon: 1) data collected and interviews of state officials and society members; and 2) research findings of care service regulations.

Education

MBA, Health Care Administration; Union College, Schenectady, New York, 1991.

BA, Sociology; cum laude; Union College, Schenectady, New York, 1990.

Professional Affiliations

American College of Healthcare Executives
Alpha Kappa Delta Sociology Honor Society

NOTES

Let's review this sample.

University students often tell me they don't have enough real-world work experience to develop a traditional resume. Or they feel their experience may not relate to what employers are looking for. The student who wrote this resume was in such a situation. When she first approached me about developing her resume, she was concerned about making herself marketable to health care organizations when she didn't have experience. This was a major concern especially with the competition for jobs from professionals who do have experience. So, her task was to figure out how to present herself so a prospective employer would want to schedule an interview.

This graduate student had prepared a typical resume with:

- College major and degrees listed first;
- Two columns listing related courses and grade-point average;
- Descriptions of academic awards, fraternal organizations, sports activities, hobbies, etc.; and
- A final section that listed part-time jobs by name and location.

All this information is interesting, but just how relevant is it to a hiring manager, especially considering the 15-second rule?

Instead, I asked her to list every school project, assignment and activity she could remember. She thought of several major projects for which she was a team member. She also remembered her two internships. Remember my two favorite questions?

1. *What did you do when you did that?;* and

2. *So what?*

Well, I asked them. Once my client started thinking about what she had been involved with in each project and internships, the information began flowing onto the paper. It hadn't occurred to her to think about the work she had done on school projects or as a college intern as being "real work." Once she started thinking in these terms, it was easy to itemize those tasks and projects she had been involved in and to identify the related skills that employers will find marketable. It didn't occur to her to identify the skills she used in the school projects.

The result of her hard work is the resume just shown. I remember vividly her comment when we finished the resume – "I didn't realize how much I had accomplished during school. I really DO have skills that an employer will find useful." Her confidence exploded and she was ready to begin her job search – to network and get job interviews. We talked about how she should target entry-level positions as a way of getting started.

With this focus, my client was able to get multiple interviews within two months and she turned down her first job offer because it didn't match her career goals. She accepted a second job offer.

My advice to all undergraduate and graduate students: Seriously analyze every part-time job, internship, school project and assignment you've accomplished. Ask yourself "What did I do when I was involved in that project?" Your response to this question will help you identify accomplishments, skills and achievements employers are looking for. Once identified, match those skills and accomplishments to an employer's needs.

Sample resume: Director of nursing for a major community hospital

Jane Smith
1234 Ivy Street
Denver, CO   80000
(303) 555 - 1212

Professional Summary

More than 18 years experience in surgery, including nine years dedicated to progressive leadership positions; three as director of surgery on a 19- suite surgery department, PACU and Pre-op area; six years experience as a nurse manager of a nine-room department.

Qualifications

- Surgery development, orientation and competencies.
- Liaison among administration, physicians,and surgical staff.
- Financial planning and budgeting in a complex hospital environment.
- Program development and implementation.
- Quality improvement programs.
- Personal management.

Professional Accomplishments

- Restructured surgery department to integrate clinical requirements with expense considerations; decreased management level FTs by 40 percent and staff FTEs by 20 percent over a two-year period while surgeries increased 35 percent.

- Developed and implemented surgery-specific patient standards of care based on AORN recommendations.

- Researched, defined and proposed the purchase and integration of a surgery-specific information system. Successfully implemented the system within the department; trained staff and physicians.

- Assisted in planning the remodeling and expansion of inpatient surgery suites and support areas; instrumental in planning of a new nine-room ambulatory surgery center.

- Opened six off-site surgical suites that expanded overall capacity and improved patient access.

- Directed preoperative nurse programs to meet staffing needs.

- Coordinated shared risk alliance with supply partners that realized cost savings of over $400,000 per year.

- Redesigned surgery support areas to provide greater patient access and more rapid turnaround times.

- Streamlined the orthopedic prosthetic vendors from ten to three primaries via physician consensus and peer review resulting in annual cost savings of $240,000.

Professional Experience

Denver Community Hospital   **1994 - 1997**
Denver, Colorado
Director of Surgery

Denver Community Hospital is a 600-bed, not-for-profit acute care facility. The inpatient OR is a 21-suite department that accommodates all subspecialties with the exception of transplant and trauma. Center performs approximately 12,000 procedures a year.

Mountain States Medical Center   **1988 - 1994**
Denver, Colorado
Nurse Manager, Operating Room

Mountain States Medical Center is a 400-bed, not-for-profit community medical center with inpatient OR consisting of nine multispecialty surgical suites. A strong emphasis on orthopedic/sports medicine, GYN and endosopic procedures. Medical center performs approximately 6000 procedures per year.

Colorado Memorial Hospital   **1977 - 1988**
Denver, Colorado
Staff Nurse, OR

Colorado Memorial Hospital is a 300 bed city owned hospital charged with providing quality health care to the indigent population. It is a multi-specialty hospital and a nationally recognized level 1 trauma center as well as a significant teaching facility; a primary site for the University residency program.

Education

Master of Science: Nursing Administration; Regis University; Denver, Colorado; 1993.

Bachelor of Science: Nursing; Loretto Heights College; Denver, Colorado; 1988.

Diploma in Nursing; Brockton Hospital School of Nursing; Brockton, MA; 1974.

Licensure and Certification

RN License No. 11111
CNOR Certification

Professional Affiliations

Association of Operating Room Nurses

Let's review this sample. Notice the different format of this resume. First, it has a professional summary and qualifications section. Second, it presents accomplishments followed by work experience. In this format, you are able to focus the employer on specific accomplishments, not on organizations. You can use accomplishments that best match the needs of the employer and highlight them on the first page while de-emphasizing the organizations and dates by leaving them to the second or third page. It's a hybrid format, not really chronological or functional. Third, it omits the objective statement.

Sample resume: Chronological format customized to a position for a senior financial operations manager

John Adams
3333 Smith Avenue
Chico, CA 99999
Home (303) 555 - 1212
Fax (303) 555 - 1313

Objective

Senior Financial Operations Manager: Multi-Specialty Health Care Programs, Services and Operations

Qualifications

More than 15 years experience in operations, accounting, management planning, analysis and cost control development for two leading health care organizations. Expertise includes financial and project management, budget preparation, analysis and control, cash processing, provider reimbursement and workers' compensation.

Professional Experience

South Pacific Medical Center   **1993 - Present**
Los Angeles, CA
Department Business Manager/Administration & Finance Coordinator

Directed business management functions of the Plant Operations Department responsible for construction and maintenance activities of a 1,200 bed acute-care medical center with more than 5,000 employees and 2 million covered square feet of medical space. Duties included cost accounting and financial planning, administrative support activities, computer systems development and interface with purchasing, accounting, legal, grants and special funding, outside contractors, vendors and regulatory agencies.

- Managed the development and implementation of a cost accounting project management system . Goal was to control $50 million in construction projects in process. Established financial controls and time line planning to report detailed project status of project teams to medical center board and administration. Used Windows/NT client server technology.

- Provided financial tools that enabled project managers to develop and monitor complex projects and systems; reduce overall capital expenditures. Result: Reduced total project costs $3.5 million in the first year.

- Established cost center budgetary reporting and operational review process for supervisors and managers. Included monthly detail variance analysis that provided line item control over $15 million in annual cost center related expenditures.

- Centralized control over administrative functions and technical support activities. Result: Internal work duplication significantly reduced and overall staffing expenses lowered 25 percent.

West Coast Medical Group of California   **1975 - 1993**
Desert Valley, CA
Director of Accounting Operations

Directed risk management functions and claim payment auditors for managed care and various member groups with regard to claim over-payment recovery and collection, workers' compensation and third-party liability operations. Prepared monthly statements of financial results, general ledger control, journal entries and account reconciliation. Investigated and corrected accounting and claim system problems through close coordination with the claims payment units, membership, systems analysis and corporate audit departments. Also managed hospital/professional reimbursement along with the cashiering and bank reconciliation functions.

- Increased recoveries in claim errors and workers' compensation liens by $5 million representing a 30 percent improvement over established goals. This translated to lower annual premium rates to member groups and improved group retention.

- Increased monthly financial recoveries of claim payment errors from $18,000 to more than $100,000 by requiring more detailed researching of transactions in claim processing, membership, eligibility, co-insurance and medical review.

- Developed a stand-alone PC based reporting system for controlling accounts receivable work-in-process inventory using dBase and Clipper programming.

Northwest Community Hospital   **1973 - 1975**
Santa Barbara, CA
Hospital Controller

Managed accounting and financial activities of a 150-bed acute care hospital. Maintained financial reporting to corporate staff, state and federal regulatory agencies, insured the financial integrity and met monthly profitability goals. Developed monthly financial statements, source and use of funds, monthly forecast of cash and profit and loss statements. Prepared account reconciliation, monthly departmental profit variance analysis and general ledger review. Worked closely with ancillary and service related departments. Also managed the business office, admitting and central supply functions.

- Developed a quarterly program of internal audit and control that insured conformity with generally accepted accounting policies and procedures.

- Increased timeliness and accuracy of monthly accounting and financial reporting to corporate management.

- Improved accounts receivable recoveries by 25 percent by revising business office follow-up procedures and how outside vendor agencies were used.

Education

Master of Business Administration; University of Southern California; Los Angeles, CA

Bachelor of Science - Business & Accounting; UCLA; Los Angeles, CA.

Related Education

Healthcare Financial Management Association courses in managed care and hospital accounting.

University extension courses in ICD9CM/ CPT/RVS coding and insurance billing.

Computer skills: Solomon Project Accounting, Excel, Word, Windows 95, Windows 3.1, DOS, dBase, Lotus 1-2-3, Access and Microsoft Project.

Affiliations

- Institute of Management Accountants
- Healthcare Financial Management Association
- Planning Executives Institute

Some observations you could make about this sample resume:

1. Notice the lengthy descriptive paragraphs following each job title. In this case, this person listed in paragraph form a few duties or responsibilities and accomplishments, then included only three or four bulleted accomplishments.

2. Notice how the accomplishment statements are actually two or three sentences. These are examples of the stories you need to write describing each task or project you've completed.

3. Note how this resume was customized for a large medical center or hospital. How could this person have toned down his information had he responded to a multi-specialty group with 15 physicians and affiliated with a local hospital? One way would be to omit the dollar figures. These large dollar figures might lead a hiring manager of a smaller group practice to screen this person out. Why? Well, the hiring manager may perceive that this individual would not be happy, long term, in a smaller group where the scope of business is much smaller. But this candidate **may** be looking for a smaller group on purpose and thinking that using larger dollar figures would be a plus.

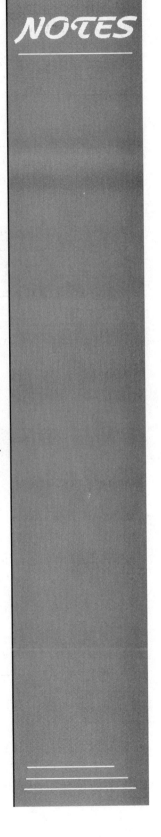

Preparing your resume for electronic scanning

Processing resumes and applications by computer is very popular. Referred to as electronic applicant tracking, it's especially popular with recruiters and is becoming a trend with healthcare organizations. Many are now posting job vacancies on their Internet web page. Thousands of applicants are using the Internet as a job-search tool.

I don't intend to discuss electronic scanning in detail. My purpose is to introduce you to the idea and encourage you to explore your local bookstores for resources.

Electronic scanning

When your resume is scanned, computer software reads the text and extracts key information including your name, address, phone number, work experience, skills and education/certifications. The software sorts your information into sections, then extracts information from each section for comparison with the search criteria for a particular job. For example, information could be sorted into functional categories like managed care, management, finance, human resources, engineering, accounting, administration, single-specialty, multi-specialty, etc. The list is endless. A first "cut" would be done by computer based on the functional areas critical to the open position.

Resumes are also scanned for skills. If a hospital wanted to hire an administrator to manage a department, the search criteria could be administration or manager and skills including budgeting, organizing, planning, staffing, etc.

Scanners will translate only the data they can understand and recognize. The best way to ensure that a scanner will "understand" the words on your resume is to lay it out in a format

that is easy for the scanner to read. To successfully prepare your resume for scanning, think
about mechanics and content.

Mechanics

Follow these tips to help ensure a computer reads
your resume to the best extent possible:

- Any resume format can be scanned – chronological, functional or marketing letter;
- Each document page MUST be clean. When
mailing your resume, do not fold it into a
standard #10 envelope; instead mail it flat in
a large envelope. Fold lines on your paper
can create large black smudges on scanned
copies. Don't take the chance – don't fold or
staple;
- Don't count on faxed resumes to accurately
scan. Always use originals;
- Eliminate all formatting. This applies to large
or fancy fonts, graphics, lines, bolding, italics, boxes, shading and column layouts;
- Use fonts that are crisp and easy to read like
Courier, Geneva, Times New Roman and
Helvetica. For those of you using Macintosh,
Palatino works well. Font size should be 10
or 12 point;
- Use only white paper and black ink. Colored
paper and ink will not give a clear scan. Check
your toner cartridge; light copies will not scan;
- Laser printer copies provide a better image.
Don't use copies from a dot matrix printer;
and
- Include your name at the top of every page.
This is for identification if any pages get sep-
arated during scanning or handling or if the
scanning blurs.

These same requirements are also critical for
resumes read by people. Think about it – readers
scan the material and sort based on predetermined criteria.

Content

Content becomes very important when customizing a resume for scanning. During scanning, the computer "extracts" information from your resume and cover letter. Just as in a cover letter or resume that is read, you have to do your homework to learn as much as you can about the key words that will increase your opportunities for matching requirements to your resume. It's called getting "hits."

Make sure you describe your accomplishments and experience using specific, descriptive words – nouns, not vague descriptions. I've talked throughout this book about connecting with the person reviewing resumes. It's the same when preparing your resume for scanning – you've got to connect with the computer and the best way to do that is to know and understand the key requirements, the criteria for the position. Follow these guidelines:

- Know enough about the job you are applying for to use the appropriate key words to define your experience, skills and education;

- Use words that specifically describe your background. For example, use a statement like *"Negotiated three managed care contracts for the clinic"* instead of a statement like *"Responsible for managing contracts for the clinic."* In the first example, you have the chance of "hitting" on the word negotiated as well as managed care and contracts;

- Use a qualification section, instead of a professional summary. In this section you should list any specific skills or talents not mentioned or referred to in the accomplishment statements;

- Be sure to include every software programs you are proficient in; list by program name;

- Make sure that accomplishment and achievement statements include key words that link to the important requirements and qualifications found in the position; and

- Include technical terms; industry jargon; certifications and licenses; degrees.

When scanned, your resume will be selected only if enough key words are found – the qualifications and minimum requirements of the position. These words are usually nouns or short descriptive phrases. Nouns describe your specific qualifications, skills, knowledge and abilities.

Examples of nouns that could trigger the computer scan are:

> Managed care director
> Group administrator
> Accountant
> Operations
> Auxiliary services
> Clinic administration
> Finance director
> Human resources
> Practice manager
> Oral and written communications
> Chief financial officer

Do your research to uncover the appropriate nouns and phrases to use in your cover letter and resume that will have the best chance of MATCHING those the employer used to describe that position.

Do your research to determine key words. Of course, you will find many sources to help you identify the key words:

- The job announcement will outline specific job requirements or duties – these directly relate to key words;

- An announcement may refer to specific qualifications and be listed as required skills and/or desired skills. These are excellent hints as to key words to use;

NOTES

- A position description will also list qualifications, job duties, education requirements, etc. – each an excellent source of key words; and

- One-on-one discussions with a hiring manager or an human resource representative will also provide hints as to key words. In this case, however, ask the right questions.

There are other sources. How many can you think of?

Don't confuse key words with the verbs, the action words you've used to begin each accomplishment statement in your resume data base. Key words are probably not these verbs.

Your job is to identify as many of those key words (qualifications and requirements) as you can and then customize your resume and cover letter, to specifically use those words. You may have the skills and background but, if the right words are not used, you may be overlooked by the computer.

Once the computer has picked your resume as a match with minimum qualifications, hiring managers or recruiters then will conduct the typical assessment of the resume – to determine if you'll be called for an interview. They want to determine what you can do for them (previous achievements) and how well you can do it (results or outcomes of previous work).

So, your resume must still be visually perfect – formatted in the way described earlier in this chapter, visually pleasing to the human eye and easy for readers to quickly match your experience and background with their needs. Remember the 15-second rule, it still applies.

Here's a chronological resume that's formatted for computer screening. A functional resume would use the same format. Notice how close it is to the typical resume I've discussed earlier:

Example of resume customized for electronic scanning

John Adams
3333 Smith Avenue
Chico, CA 99999
Home (303) 555 - 1212

Objective Statement

Senior Financial Operations Manager

Professional Summary (Qualifications)

A senior financial operations manager for a multi-speciality group with over 15 years experience in operations, accounting, management planning, analysis and cost control development. Financial & project management. Budget preparation for $35 million annual budget. Cash processing. Provider reimbursement and workers' compensation.

Professional Experience

Department Business Manager/Administration & Finance Coordinator
1993 - Present
South Pacific Medical Center, Los Angeles, CA

Directed business management functions of the Operations Department responsible for construction and maintenance activities of a 1,200 bed acute-care medical center with more than 5,000 employees and 2 million covered square feet of medical space. Duties included cost accounting and financial planning, administrative support activities, computer systems development and interface with purchasing, accounting, legal, grants and special funding, outside contractors, vendors and regulatory agencies.

Significant Accomplishments:

-   Managed the development and implementation of a cost accounting project management system. Established financial controls and time line planning to report detailed project status of project teams to medical center board and administration.

-   Provided financial tools that enabled project managers to develop and monitor complex projects and systems; reduce overall capital expenditures. Result: Reduced total project costs $3.5 million in the first year.

- Established cost center budgetary reporting and operational review process for supervisors and managers. Included monthly detail variance analysis that provided line item control over $15 million in annual cost center related expenditures.

- Centralized control over administrative functions and technical support activities. Result: Internal work duplication significantly reduced and overall staffing expenses lowered 25 percent.

Director of Accounting Operations   1975 - 1993
West Coast Medical Group of California;
Desert Valley, CA

Directed risk management functions and claim payment auditors for managed care and various member groups with regard to claim over-payment recovery and collection, workers' compensation and third-party liability operations. Prepared monthly statements of financial results, general ledger control, journal entries and account reconcilia-tion. Investigated and corrected accounting and claim system prob-lems through close coordination with the claims payment units, mem-bership, systems analysis and corporate audit departments. Managed hospital/professional reimbursement along with the cashiering and bank reconciliation functions.

Significant Accomplishments:

- Increased recoveries in claim errors and workers' compensation liens by $5 million representing a 30 percent improvement over established goals.

- Increased monthly financial recoveries of claim payment errors from $18,000 to more than $100,000 by requiring more detailed researching of transactions in claim processing, membership, eli-gibility, co-insurance and medical review.

- Developed a stand-alone PC based reporting system for controlling accounts receivable work-in-process inventory using dBase and Clipper programming.

Hospital Controller   1973 - 1975
Northwest Community Hospital
Santa Barbara, CA

Managed accounting and financial activities of a 150-bed acute care hospital. Maintained financial reporting to corporate staff, state and federal regulatory agencies, insured the financial integrity and met monthly profitability goals. Developed monthly financial statements, source and use of funds, monthly forecast of cash and profit and loss statements. Prepared account reconciliation, monthly departmental profit variance analysis and general ledger review. Worked closely with ancillary and service related departments. Also managed the business office, admitting and central supply functions.

Significant Accomplishments:

-   Developed a quarterly program of internal audit and control that insured conformity with generally accepted accounting policies and procedures.

-   Increased timeliness and accuracy of monthly accounting and financial reporting to corporate management.

-   Improved accounts receivable recoveries by 25 percent by revising business office follow-up procedures and how outside vendor agencies were used.

Education

Master of Business Administration; University of Southern California; Los Angeles, CA.

Bachelor of Science - Business & Accounting; UCLA; Los Angeles, CA.

Professional Affiliations & Related Education

Institute of Management Accountants
Medical Group Management Association
Healthcare Financial Management Association
Planning Executives Institute

Healthcare Financial Management Association courses in managed care and hospital accounting.

University extension courses in ICD9CM/CPT/ RVS coding and insurance billing.

Computer skills: Solomon Project Accounting, Excel, Word, Windows 95, Windows 3.1, DOS, dBase, Lotus 1-2-3, Access and Microsoft Project.

Conclusion

You don't need to do any major modifications to your resume or cover letter to prepare them for computer scanning. Your objective is still to uncover needs and identify qualifications. Then customize them to match those requirements – using key words or phrases. Only the formatting is different.

The major differences are:

1. All formatting is eliminated including bolding and italics. Shift all information to the left margin.

2. Use key words and technical jargon to increase the number of "hits" when scanned.

Now it's your turn

Put these ideas to work.

I bet you've omitted accomplishments from your resume in order to maintain the two-page rule. Now that I've destroyed that myth, create your resume database. Include every accomplishment and achievement you can think of. Don't leave any out. Tell your success "story" for each one.

Use this database to customize every cover letter and resume you use from this point on.

I'd love to review your progress and answer any questions. My phone number and e-mail address are in Chapter 1.

Take charge of your selling tools II: write letters that enhance your job search

Your ability to communicate effectively by letter is critical to a successful job search. Often, your letter is the first contact a potential employer has with you, and first impressions are critical. Hiring managers may form perceptions when reading your cover letter that affect their decisions on whether to screen you in or out. This chapter reviews types of written correspondence and shows how important they are to your job search. Specifically, I'll review cover letters that accompany your resume, letters to use as a follow-up to information and job interviews, and thank-you notes, including those you should send if you received a rejection. You'll learn formats and wording for cover letters, and we'll review a few critical guidelines for all written correspondence.

Writing letters to accompany your resume

Don't underestimate the power of a well-conceived and written cover letter. To write a powerful letter, start by thinking of it as the FIRST page of your resume. Remember, the person who screens resumes usually makes the first decision in 15 seconds, which includes time to scan your cover letter and connect with you.

In most situations, the reader won't know you or your background. You want your cover letter to present a favorable impression of you and your qualifications while reflecting the real YOU. So, write naturally and make sure you consider the five sections in all effective cover letters:

1. Establish purpose to grab the reader's attention;
2. Hold the reader's attention;
3. Respond to a request for salary history and requirements (if needed); and
4. Cover your follow-up and next steps; and
5. Close.

Let's review each of these sections.

Grab the reader's attention

Your opening sentence must interest your reader immediately. An opening sentence like:

Enclosed herewith please find my resume for the position of . . .

won't interest anyone. In fact, it may lull readers into complacency, thinking to themselves, "Here I go again, another dull letter. It's only the tenth one I've read today." Instead, sound enthusiastic, motivated and interested in the position. Here are some examples:

• Based on your growth and expansion history, my experience and contributions are a perfect match for your medical group;

• Based on my research, your medical group looks like one that will be interested in my background and experience;

• I'm very interested in the _____ opportunity you recently described in the _____. I know that I meet the qualifications for the position and believe I would be an excellent candidate;

• Regarding your recent advertisement in the _____ for a _____, I'm confident you will be interested in my experience and background; and

• Three areas of the _____ position you advertised suggest I am the person you're looking for.

174

Hold the reader's attention

Even though this section includes the "meat" of your cover letter, keep it short and to the point. You hold a reader's attention by selling accomplishments that directly relate to needs – to the position's requirements. A reader will appreciate your getting right to the point; so many cover letters beat around the bush with extraneous, irrelevant information. Use one of the following models to form this section of your letter:

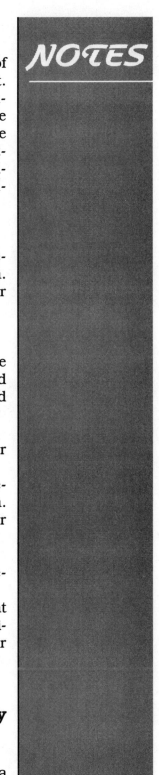

*   My qualifications include:
        (List four or five accomplishment statements that relate directly to the position. It's okay to repeat bullets from your resume.);

*   Specifically, I have:
        (Indicate number of years experience that matches the position's needs and bullet specific experiences, skills and accomplishments.);

*   My career accomplishments that match your requirements are:
        (List four or five accomplishment statements that relate directly to the position. It's okay to repeat bullets from your resume;) and

*   My recent accomplishments and achievements include:
        (Again, list of four or five accomplishment statements that relate directly to the position. It's okay to repeat bullets from your resume.).

Respond to a request for salary history or requirements

Rule-of-thumb: Don't provide a salary figure in a cover letter. Organizations ask this question to weed out inappropriate candidates – they decide

to screen you in or out based solely on salary requirements before investing time and energy in an interview. Three things can happen when you include a salary figure, and two are negative:

1. You're screened out because your stated salary requirements are higher than what the company wants to pay. You may be viewed as "too experienced" for the position;

2. You're screened out because your salary requirements are too low. You're viewed as not experienced enough "to do what we're looking for"; or

3. Your salary requirement just happens to fall within the company's range – pure luck.

Once in a while you'll find an ad that reads: *only applications with salary requirements or history will be considered*. In this case, provide a salary figure and live with the consequences. But first, do some research to help you estimate the organization's likely compensation package or find industry standards for comparable positions. Sources are available; you just have to be creative and find them.

Believe it or not, the most obvious solution to this problem is often the easiest – call the organization and ask for the salary range or compensation for this position. Organizations will usually tell you.

Other research you can do:

•   Seek out and ask representatives from similar organizations what their salary range or compensation package is for related positions;

•   Review publications like the *Occupational Outlook Handbook* (in your local library). It provides typical earnings for related positions;

•   Review various survey reports on salary or compensation. For example, the Medical Group Management Association provides an annual study of management compensation and reports on academic practice management compensation; and

- Ask people in your network. They may be aware of potential salary ranges.

To avoid stating an exact salary figure, try using one of the following statements when a classified ad asks for salary figures. Most of the hiring managers I've talked with about this issue say that a response like one of these is acceptable; it wouldn't screen you out:

1. "My salary requirements are flexible depending on the position's responsibilities and requirements";

2. "Before providing a meaningful salary figure, I'd like to discuss with you this position's responsibilities and opportunities"; or

3. "My salary has continuously advanced in parallel with the level of responsibility and authority of my previous positions. My salary requirements are flexible depending on the responsibilities and objectives of the group practice."

Your follow-up and next steps

Here's another critical part of your cover letter – it helps you maintain control of your job search. Always state a follow-up action you will take. Many cover letters miss this opportunity by ending with something like:

I look forward to hearing from you at your earliest possible convenience.

Ask yourself, what kind of action does this statement encourage the reader to take? The answer – nothing! Besides, you end up waiting for a response. After two or three weeks, when you still haven't heard anything, you write it off as another lost opportunity.

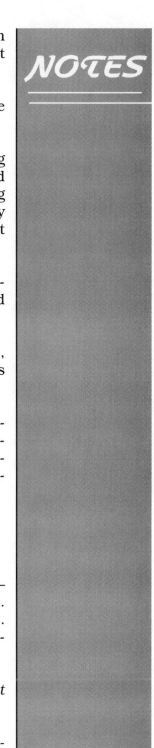

Instead, I suggest a statement that should catch the reader's attention. Use a concluding statement that gives you permission to call the organization – not wait for them to call:

1. "I'll call you within five working days to see how we should proceed";

2. "I'll call you on Tuesday the 14th to see if you have further questions about my background and to arrange a time to get together";

3. "I plan to be near your office next week. I'll call to see if we might meet for 15 minutes to discuss my background and how it matches your requirements; or

4. "I plan to be in your area next week and would like to get together either Thursday or Friday for 15 minutes to discuss my qualifications."

Of course, when you use a statement like this, you MUST call when you said you would. As soon as you finish the cover letter, put a reminder note in your daily schedule book for the day and time you're to call. My experience is that organizations react favorably to this approach. As a candidate, you're taking initiative and showing volition – traits that executives like in employees. Executives like people who take charge – and there's no better place to demonstrate your ability to take charge than in a cover letter. Remember, it's the first impression someone has of you.

Closing

End your cover letter on an upbeat note. You may spend considerable time crafting the perfect cover letter but often ruin the ending. An ending like *"Thank you for your time and consideration"* is all too common. But it just sits there; it doesn't do anything to motivate the reader. *"Very truly yours"* or *"sincerely"* are as bad because they're overused.

Your cover letter can be business-like and still communicate warmth and a personal touch. You have to sense the character of your audience and write accordingly. I feel it's better to be too warm than too formal or distant, so make a good impression with an ending like:

1. *"Enthusiastically"* or

2. *"Best wishes, always"*

Identifying an employer's needs from a classified ad: A case study

Classified ads contain a wealth of information – if you look for it. Review the following classified ad. What information could you use from the ad to craft a cover letter that matches your experience with the organization's needs?

Managed Care Director

Progressive, Northeast-based MSO seeks an individual to supervise and coordinate managed care contracts for various clients. Ideal candidate should have excellent written and verbal skills; analytical and financial skills; strategic planning skills; knowledge and understanding of contract negotiations.

A bachelor's degree in Health or Business Administration required; master's degree preferred.

We offer a competitive, generous benefit package. Qualified candidates should forward resumes with salary requirements in confidence to – Fax #: (303) 555 - 1212, attention Human Resource Department.

Inappropriate responses

Typically, people see an ad like this in the Sunday paper – maybe even in the early edition on

Saturday afternoon. Or perhaps they've scanned the *MGM Update* or the MGMA web page. Of course, their first reaction is to submit a resume as quickly as possible. They scurry around, take their standard cover letter, change the mailing address, print out a copy of their "one-size-fits-all" resume, and send the materials off. Of course, they know they'll get a positive response because this opportunity is a perfect match for them. An interview is inevitable.

Suppose you were one of these people. After two or three weeks reality sets in. You haven't heard from anyone, positively or negatively. You're wondering what happened – why no response? You may be feeling just a little frustrated because you KNEW this was the perfect job. What do you do now? You can't even call anyone because you don't have a name or address – just a fax number. You could send another fax to the same number requesting someone call you back – but that seems just a little desperate. You're stuck and at the organization's mercy.

To see how this type of letter looks, consider how one of my clients responded to this ad. He didn't get a response – not even a negative one:

Date

Attention: Human Resource Department

RE: Managed Care Director

To whom it may concern.

Attached please find a copy of my resume. I am currently finishing a Master's degree program at the University of Colorado in health services administration. This degree will be completed fall semester 1998.

As you can see from my resume, I have a Bachelor's degree from the Colorado State University in Accounting and Business Administration.

Upon obtaining my degree, I immediately went to work for Primeria Health Care in Denver, CO. I spend 2 years at Primeria and learned a great deal about the insurance and managed care industries. But seeing greater potential, I left that position to be the finance director and assistant administrator at the Denver Medical Center in Denver.

After 18 months at the Medical Center, I was offered a position as the administrator of the Western Colorado Medical Group in Colorado Springs. Now that I am near the completion of my Master's degree in health administration, I feel that it is time to increase my professional responsibilities. I would be interested in learning more about the position of Managed Care Director. I am available for interviews the majority of the time. I look forward to hearing from you.

Sincerely:

Will an employer gain a clear understanding, in 15 seconds or less, of this person's experience with managed care? What would you do, as a screener, when you finished reading? Would you even finish reading this letter? Yet, this person believed he was a good match for the job, having experience in each of the four critical need areas. Did his cover letter demonstrate this match? No, not at all. In fact, this letter helped screen him out because:

1. The salutation didn't "grab" the reader's attention. He simply used the limited information provided in the ad. He addressed it to the "human resource department" and "To whom it may concern";

2. The opening sentence didn't excite anyone. In fact, it's obvious that his resume is attached;

3. The second sentence may have sent his application to the screen-out bin. It surely won't hold the reader's attention. Why? It focused on education and degrees, not on matching experience with needs, in this case, managed care experience;

4) The middle part of the letter is dull and wasted; and

5) Finally, the open-ended conclusion is poor. In this case, it was the only ending that could be used because this person doesn't know who to follow-up with.

A different approach

A more proactive approach takes more work – even some proficient "Sherlock Holmes detecting" but the results are worth it. Let's look at the ad in more detail to see how it can help you customize your cover letter and resume. Customizing and writing actively will enable you to connect with the reader in that critical first 15 seconds. Again, here's the text of the ad:

Managed Care Director

Progressive, Northeast-based MSO seeks an individual to supervise and coordinate managed care contracts for various clients. Ideal candidate should have excellent written and verbal skills; analytical and financial skills; strategic planning skills; knowledge and understanding of contract negotiations.

A bachelor's degree in Health or Business Administration required; master's degree preferred.

We offer a competitive, generous benefit package. Qualified candidates should forward resumes with salary requirements in confidence to – Fax #: (303) 555 - 1212, attention Human Resource Department.

What is helpful? The ad:

* Identifies the group's needs;

* Reveals that it is a blind ad, with only a fax number. Yes, even this is important information;

* Asks for salary requirements; and

* Says you can fax the resume.

Let's consider these features in turn.

Identify the group's needs.

The quickest and easiest way to customize a cover letter is to use the major requirements that are in every classified ad. In this case the important needs of the Management Service Organization (MSO) are: 1) managed care contracts; 2) analytical and financial skills; 3) strategic planning skills; and 4) knowledge and understanding of contract negotiations. These four areas are what you refer to in your customized cover letter to THIS group – in this cover letter, not in any other.

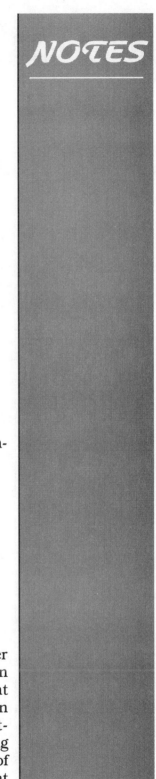

Respond to the request for salary requirements.

This request allows you to use one of the suggested responses (discussed before) instead of citing a salary range. Remember, you don't want to be screened out because you list too high, or too low, a number. Sometimes the organization will state that any resumes without salary requirements or history will not be considered unless a number is included. In this case, you should provide a salary figure that you feel comfortable with and live with the results.

Fax resumes.

Faxing resumes is now common practice. But, whenever you fax a cover letter or resume, also mail a follow-up copy. Some fax copies omit the top or bottom lines; sometimes lines are smudged or in other ways unreadable. In the example above, you have no mailing address. In this case, fax a request to the group asking them to provide a mailing address so you can follow the fax with an original copy. This serves two purposes: 1) the group gets a clean, readable copy; and 2) you put your name and material in front of them a second time.

Respond to blind ad with a telephone number.

Now you can really use your Sherlock Holmes skills. Referring to our previous examples, how could you find a group's or organization's name and address? Could you find one? I think you may be able to, with a little detective work and some luck.

First, you have the area code for the fax number. If you request an address, and they provide one, your detective work is done. If they don't, go to your telephone book and find that area code. Once you've pinpointed a region, see if you have contacts in that area. If you do, call them; see if they know of an MSO that is looking for a director of managed care. If they do, great! Ask them for a contact name and telephone number. Call the group – in this case the MSO – and say, "I understand you may have a position open for a director of managed care. Is that correct?" When they say yes, you say, "I might be interested in applying. Would you be able to tell me about the position – its duties, responsibilities, goals and objectives. This information will help me prepare my materials." Then you LISTEN, LISTEN, LISTEN. The information they provide will be what you match to your accomplishments. End the discussion by paraphrasing to the person "So, if I understand you correctly, the five major responsibilities for this job are . . . ." If this happens, congratulations – you've graduated from gumshoe to a first-rate detective.

If your detective work is not this successful, your second step is to get the MGMA's membership directory for that state and region. Contact someone from that list and ask the same questions.

If either of these approaches works, you can now send your cover letter and resume to a real person – to the person you talked to and who now knows about you. It's more personal when you can address your materials to a specific person and begin your cover letter with "The information you gave me on October 23 helped me understand that the group needs . . . . ." Or "Thank you for taking the time to talk with me. The information you provided on the 23rd was very valuable . . . ."

If you can't locate the MGMA membership list, start turning over rocks to find someone in that area who may be able to point you in the right direction. Believe me, it's worth the effort. With a little work, you can find the information you need.

So, here's how your cover letter might look if you were successful at uncovering a contact person.

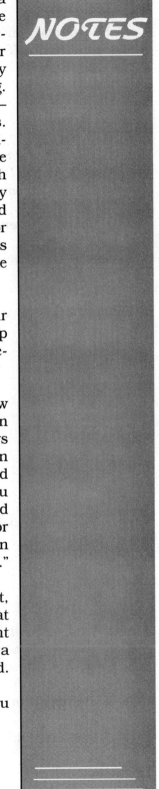

NOTES

Date

Dr. John Adams, CEO
Physicians Group MSO
1234 Main Street
Boston, MA 02222

Dear Dr. Adams:

Thank you for the time you spent with me on October 23 discussing your requirements for the Director of Managed Care position. I know you will be interested in my accomplishments and experience:

Your Requirements	**My Qualifications**
• Supervise & coordinate managed care contracts	• Managed 7 different managed-care contracts over four years.
• Contract negotiations	• Negotiated and wrote managed-care contracts with companies throughout the East Coast; monitored and initiated changes to benefit the group.
• Analytical & financial skills	• Provided financial tools to enable department heads to better monitor and control budgets and financial analysis; reduced expenses 25%.
• Strategic-planning skills	• Managed strategic planning for the group; planned and led semi-annual strategic-planning sessions; monitored ongoing plans; revised as necessary.

I know I would contribute strongly to your organization, especially with my four years of experience in negotiating and monitoring managed-care contracts. Your ad asked for salary requirements. Before providing a meaningful salary figure, I'd like to discuss in more detail the responsibilities and opportunities this position presents.

I will call you on Friday, November 10 to see how we should proceed.

Enthusiastically;
Jan Johnson MSHA

Let's review the strong points of this letter. Notice:

1. How this letter builds from the phone contact into an immediate comparison of needs and qualifications in a way that allows the reader to grasp how you match with the requirements in less than 15 seconds. You actually help the reader decide if you are a match. This is especially useful if the screener is someone from a human resource department. HR typically screens for how candidates match with minimum qualifications;

2. How you use the exact same words as used in the ad or provided by the person during your phone discussion. It's important to use "jargon" statements;

3. How the qualification statements, which are accomplishment statements from your resume, are a direct match to the job requirements. Requirements translate into needs;

4. The response to the request for salary information. No figures were used;

5. The action phrase "contributed strongly" used in the paragraph following the columns. This will catch the reader's attention and, just in case it was forgotten, it reminds the reader of your strongest accomplishment – in this case its the managed-care experience;

6. How the letter ends with a specific action that YOU will take. Give yourself permission to follow up. Schedule a time when you will call;

7. The closure – a word like "enthusiastically" is uplifting to the reader. It's not boring or routine; and

8. Finally, all this in only one page.

In conclusion – your only goal is to connect with the reader in 15 seconds so that your application gets "screened-in."

Strong letters

- Make match to needs.

- Use exact words.

- Match requirements.

- Respond about salary.

- Emphasize strengths.

Some additional samples of cover letters for different situations

1. Letter responding to a face-to-face or phone interview

2. Letter following up a face-to-face or phone interview

3. Marketing letter format in response to a classified ad

Letter responding to a face-to-face or phone interview

Dear Mr. Adams:

After discussing the needs of the Whitewater Medical Center, PC, with you, I believe I'm well qualified for the Administrator position. I know you will be interested in my accomplishments and experience:

Your Requirements	*My Qualifications*
1) *Physician recruitment*	1) *Recruited four family practice and five internal medicine physicians over the past five years.*
2) *Managed-care contracting*	2) *Negotiated and wrote managed-care contracts with companies throughout the East Coast.*
3) *Facility construction*	3) *Responsible for the planning, development and construction team that added 25,000 sq. ft. to facility.*
4) *Community involvement*	4) *Chaired the United Way campaign; worked closely with the community Outreach and Wellness program.*

I know I would contribute strongly to your organization, especially with my experience in modernizing and creating a positive image at my current clinic and hospital. These changes increased our financial return.

I will call you on Friday, October 23rd to see how we should proceed.

Enthusiastically;

Jan Johnson MSHA

Letter following up a face-to-face or phone interview

Dear Mr. Adams:

Thank you for meeting with me regarding the Human Resource - Facilitator position. In light of our discussion, I feel that my background and experience best matches the position in these areas:

Your Requirements	*My Qualifications*
• *Project Team Leader*	• *Mentored a new group of employees on department objectives. Trained team members on customer service; conflict resolution; analyzing business risks. Helped team create individual development plans.*
• *Management and Leadership*	• *Did strategic and tactical planning and decision-making for 6 years; monitored compliance with business controls and procedures; assessed new business opportunities.*
• *Process Leadership*	• *Provided technical leadership and coaching to team; balanced workload; established metrics; carried out new processes.*

I have enclosed another resume. As you requested, I'm also enclosing a list of professional references, with phone numbers – including two former managers.

I'll call the two people you recommended I talk with who have led teams, so I can get more information about the position. I know that I would strongly contribute to your organization, especially with my experience leading teams through times of change and uncertainty.

After I've met with the other facilitators, I'll call you to define our next steps.

Enthusiastically;
Jan Johnson MSHA

Marketing letter format in response to a classified ad

Here's a typical classified ad:

Medical Office Administrator

An expanding surgical group on the West Coast is seeking an experienced administrator. This person will supervise practice operations including patient care services, finance, billing and collections, data processing, marketing, network development, and all personnel functions. Candidates should have a degree in business or related field, management experience in a multi-physician practice or hospital and have a high level of energy. Please send resume and salary history to Medical Group Administrator, PO Box 1234-A, San Francisco, CA 00000.

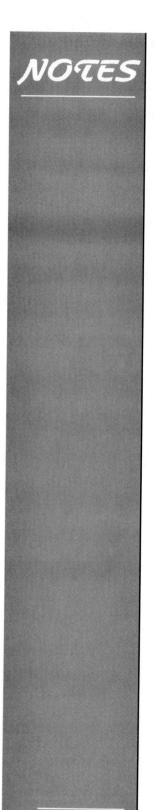

Following is an example of a cover letter written in the format of a marketing letter. Notice the layout, how the information is presented. Does it still get the point across in 15 seconds? I think it does.

Response to ad for a medical group administrator

Box 1234-A   May 15, 1999
San Francisco, CA 00000

Dear Sir or Madam:

In reviewing the Medical Group Management Update of May 12, I discovered your advertisement for a Medical Group Administrator position.

I believe you'll be interested in my accomplishments and experience:

* Established a fee-for-service billing system for two HMOs, increasing annual revenue $350,000.

* Researched and established a 401k savings plan resulting in 85-percent staff participation

* Saved the group practice more than $15,000 per year by re-negotiating supply contracts with vendors.

* Researched and installed a new computerized management information system for multiple locations, including a complete electronic data interchange for claims, payments and automated medical records.

I have enclosed my resume for your review. Your ad asked for salary requirements. Before providing a meaningful salary figure, I would like to discuss in greater detail the responsibilities and opportunities this job presents.

I know I would strongly contribute to your organization, especially considering my experience with (include a specific accomplishment statement that links to a key requirement indicated in the ad).

I'll call in a week to see how we should proceed.

Enthusiastically,

Signature

Some miscellaneous guidelines for cover letters

Here are some final thoughts about cover letters:

Purpose

- The purpose of a cover letter is to connect you with the reader. In most situations, the reader won't know you or your background. Quickly capture the reader's interest – in 15 seconds.

- Cover letters are critical because they represent you and jog memories when you're not present.

- Your letter must create a positive mental image in the reader's mind – how your background and experiences match the organization's needs.

General principles

- Always include a cover letter with a resume.

- Your cover letter is really the first page of your resume. In most cases employers screen you in or out based on the cover letter.

- Stress what you can offer, NOT what you want. Include accomplishment statements to catch the reader's interest.

- Use the company's terms whenever possible.

- Review from the reader's perspective. Make sure you present those accomplishments that best match the employer's needs.

- Make your letter perfect! Edit ruthlessly for grammar and spelling. Proofread it by reading it aloud. Ask someone else to read it.

- Say you'll call back to follow up.

- **Never** include salary information, even if the ad or person requests it.

- **Always** keep a copy.

Writing style

- Address the cover letter to an individual. If you are responding to a blind ad, or don't have a name – use "Dear Sir or Madam," or some other non-sexist salutation. In every situation, try to locate a contact person. DON'T use "To whom it may concern."

- Prepare each cover letter individually and hand sign it.

- Keep it crisp and to-the-point: only one page.

- Write naturally, the way you talk. Use active voice.

- Personalize each cover letter. Mention the individual (company) and the position you're applying for.

- Emphasize important points by underlining words (but not more than two in a row), indenting and using white space.

Thank-you notes

Thank-you notes and follow-up letters are as important to your job search as cover letters. Don't underestimate their power. Opportunities to use a thank-you or follow-up note are:

- After an informational interview;

- When you meet with a network contact;

- To summarize the results of a job interview and indicate your next steps in the hiring process;

- To thank that helpful administrative assistant or secretary who helped you when you arrived for a job interview; and

- When you receive a rejection letter.

What other situations can you think of for a good thank-you letter?

Read on for a short discussion of each opportunity.

Following up informational interviews and meetings with your networking contacts

Write a thank-you note soon after the meeting. Tell readers you'll follow up with the person or people they suggested you contact. Always keep a copy for your files.

Here's one example:

Date

Dear Ms./Mr. _____

I appreciate the courtesy you extended to me in our meeting earlier this week. Considering the demands on your schedule, it was very thoughtful.

I'm using some of your suggestions and will let you know their outcome.

(NOTE: Refer to one or two specific items from your meeting, noting any action you will take as a result of your meeting.)

Cordially,

Clients consistently ask if this type of follow-up letter could be informal and hand written. If you're writing to a person you met for the first time, I suggest a more formal approach – word-process your note. If you're writing to an acquaintance or colleague, an informal, hand-written note is fine.

Following up job interviews: a thank you to the person who interviewed you

Immediately follow-up a job interview with a short, but targeted note. By targeted, I mean to remind the interviewer of your strengths – of the one or two key ways you match their requirements. Keep the note short and crisp. Here's an example:

Date

Dear Mr./Ms./Dr.

Thanks again for the opportunity to meet and discuss your requirements for a clinic administrator.

The more I thought about our discussion, the more convinced I am about how well my previous experience with _____ *and* _____ *matches three of your critical objectives for the coming year.*

I'll call you in five working days to see what our next steps are.

In the meantime, please call if you have questions.

Cordially,

Following up with an administrative assistant or secretary

Here's an often untapped opportunity. Anytime an administrative assistant or secretary helped coordinate your job interview, send a separate, short, thank-you note. I guarantee this technique will get results.

Here's a personal example. When I interviewed with the Medical Group Management Association, the senior executives' administrative assistant was very helpful. When I arrived at MGMA's lobby, she was waiting to greet me and take me to the interview. Along the way, she quickly overviewed the Association and the offices we were passing. She provided coffee and made sure I was comfortable while I waited for the appointment. She made me feel as though I were part of the organization. After the interview, she provided background material about MGMA and scheduled a follow-up phone call.

Remember, administrative assistants and secretaries seldom, or never, receive acknowledgment for their efforts. I sent a very short note thanking her for her time and effort, stating how she had made me feel right at home.

After I had been offered the consulting contract, the senior manager said he felt almost compelled to do so because of the "input" he received from his administrative assistant. As I understand it, she showed him the note, said this was the first time she'd ever received anything like it, and strongly said I was the only logical choice. Now, I know this wasn't the only reason for the offer, but the senior executive said it was important to his final decision.

Don't ignore the power of this technique.

Thank-you note when you don't receive an offer

Thank people for not giving you an offer? Hal, are you crazy? No, just practical. From this point on, think about a rejection as another chance to add to your list of network contacts. Consider this – if you were a finalist for a position but weren't chosen, the hiring manager liked what he saw and heard. Perhaps the final decision may have come down to "personality fit," not to qualifications or skills. Consider this hiring manager an ally – someone who could and, in most cases, will provide names of colleagues you can contact. I know of several instances in which a hiring manager hadn't thought about referring a client to a colleague until my client sent a rejection thank-you letter. Hiring mangers view this technique as very professional – one more reason to recommend you to others.

Don't walk away from this valuable resource *just because you didn't get the offer.* Instead, write something like the following note to the hiring manager:

Sample follow-up note to a rejection

Dear Jim:

Just a note to thank you for the opportunity to interview with you and the Board of Ridgeway Medical Group. Though I had hoped for a different outcome, I compliment you on the thoroughness of the interview process. I'm sure the candidate you chose will bring a lot of talent and administrative skill to the job and should be an excellent manager. But I'm pleased you considered me a top candidate.

For the time being, I'm focusing my search on opportunities in Colorado. I'll call in the coming month to ask if you know of other groups in Colorado I could contact about positions or information interviews.

Many thanks.

Sincerely,

As with every thank-you and follow-up letter, be sure to make a note in your schedule book to call this person at the appropriate time. Include the phone number in your book so you don't have to look it up. A few of my clients have lost phone numbers – you don't want that to happen to you.

Cover letters and follow-up letters are a powerful tool in your job search tool kit. Don't underestimate their usefulness. Take the time to craft customized letters for every situation.

They help you get results.

NOTES

Chapter 6

Take charge of your interviews

"If you and the interviewer feel uncomfortable with each other after an hour, imagine the discomfort you'll feel after several months on the job."

Taunee Besson,
National Business Employment Weekly,
September 25, 1988

"You will never convince a future employer of your relevance and value to the organization unless you are able to relate your abilities and experiences to his/her needs."

Germann & Arnold,
Job & Career Building,
10 Speed Press, 1980

Interview realities

You've worked long and hard to get to this point. All the work you've put into preparing your resume database, developing contacts using your network, and customizing cover letters and resumes has paid off. An employer called to schedule a phone or face-to-face interview. This is a position and organization that you think is an excellent match with your career goal. Now what? You don't want to blow this opportunity. You know your performance is critical; you must impress the interviewer(s). How can you prepare yourself so you go into the interview confident of your skills and abilities? What can you do to communicate your competence to the employer and "fit" in this stressful environment?

This chapter discusses how to prepare yourself for an interview including the research you must do before you meet face-to-face with the interviewer. Preparation is critical because, no matter whether the interviewers are trained or untrained, their only task is to uncover and determine reasons *not to hire you!*

The reality is that organizations have several candidates for every position and the power to choose the person for the job. They'll eliminate any candidate who interviews poorly. Because they must decide quickly, you're in the tough position of having to make a positive and strong first impression. As a candidate, your success depends on your ability to be perceived as someone who can both fit in and help the organization and the hiring manager succeed. The hiring organization is interested in candidates who can contribute to the organization, and show significant results from previous organizations because of their skills, accomplishments and ability to fit into the organization's culture. If you don't fit the organization profile, your chances of getting an offer are slim.

Interviewing skills must be integral to your job search strategy. Preparation is critical if you are to be successful. By maintaining a positive, "I can do it" attitude, you can effectively control the job interview. Let's move you in that direction by overviewing the different types of interviews and then take you through the job-interview process:

• Preparing for the first job interview;

• Completing the first job interview;

• Dealing with the second job interview;

• Handling the third and subsequent job interviews; and

• Planning for and handling group interviews.

Understanding the types of interviews

First, we need to recognize that interviews take different forms, depending on the purpose and expected outcome. Five common types are the:

- Screening interview;

- Proposal interview;

- Referral interview;

- Information interview – an important opportunity we'll discuss in more detail; and

- Job interview – the focus of your job search and a large part of this chapter.

Screening interviews

Screening interviews compare your qualifications, skills and background with the position's minimum specifications. Usually, people in human resources or personnel departments do these interviews, but in some smaller group practices, you may interview with an administrative assistant to the chief executive officer or board chairperson. In some cases, an executive search firm may do the screening.

Because screening matches candidates to minimum qualifications, decisions could depend solely on whether a candidate has the appropriate or specific degree. Or the decision could depend on if the candidate has the minimum years of experience in a specific specialty or size of group practice.

Most screening interviewers have limited knowledge of the position and its day-to-day activities, so this isn't the time to ask technical or other specific questions. Your goal is to show you match the minimum requirements, so you can get past the screener to the person who has the power to make a decision – the hiring manager.

NOTES

Interview Types

- Screening

- Proposal

- Referral

- Information

- Job

Proposal interviews

This is a meeting you arrange with a hiring manager or someone else in the group practice who can make a hiring decision. In this interview, you actually give a sales pitch to the hiring manager, describing how your skills and background will contribute to the success of the manager and the organization. Your research and knowledge may identify areas in which their needs match your skills, experience and competencies.

An example: You have just helped maneuver your current group through a complicated, yet successful, integration with a larger health care organization. Looking for the same kind of challenge elsewhere, you may uncover another group practice just beginning a similar integration. In this case, you would go directly to the Chief Executive Officer (CEO) or board chairperson and propose how you could work as an integration specialist and manage the transition.

In this proposal interview you describe your experience, skills and outcomes of previous work; present your proposal on how you might work with them; and respond to questions or requests for further exploration and clarification.

Your goal is to "create" jobs where they may not have existed – actively helping a manager recognize a need.

Referral interviews

In a referral interview you explain to others the type of job you are looking for and ask them for advice about the best way to locate it. Your goal is to uncover job leads and openings by sharing with others your objectives and describing your qualifications and experience. You want to make a favorable impression so people will remember you and be motivated to tell you when they hear of a job opening.

A referral interview is particularly useful when you are clear about your career goal and the type of position or work you want. Referral interviews often develop from information interviews – an important source of opportunities discussed in more detail later.

During a referral interview you want to:

*   Establish rapport with the person you're meeting. Without personal i n v o l v e m e n t from your contact, nothing else happens;
*   Find out what jobs or opportunities exist;
*   Continue adding to your network list; and
*   Be sure the person you're talking with remembers you and is willing to help in your job search. You also must agree to keep this person informed of your progress and results.

When setting up a referral interview, be sure to tell people why you chose them; if anyone referred you to them; your current employment situation; the exact purpose in asking for a referral interview; and your career goal or objective.

But don't imply you expect them to have, or to know of, a job opening.

Information interviews

This is a very effective technique you can use to uncover information and related opportunities within your network. It's a short (20 - 30 minutes) interview with a person who has a similar job and responsibilities. Your goal is to find out as much as you can about a particular job or profession. The data will help you decide if it matches your career interests and goals. People who work in a job can give you down-to-earth information that will help you decide whether you can achieve your goal or must modify it.

An information interview is different from a job interview in that nearly all questions are acceptable. In a job interview you don't want to ask

NOTES

some questions or feel you can't ask them until an appropriate time. Examples are questions that deal with salary, strengths and weaknesses. These types of questions are appropriate in an information interview.

This approach works because the people you interview aren't under pressure to find you a job or hire you; they are simply providing you information you need to make career– related decisions. Information interviews allow you to educate yourself about a job or organization.

Think of yourself as a "private eye" investigating career fields or potential organizations. This approach will uncover volumes of useful information and new network contacts.

Setting up an information interview

First:

* Identify the profession, job or field you're interested in exploring.

* Research organizations in your areas of interest using personal contacts, library sources, annual reports, brochures, trade associations and journals, and articles from magazines and newspapers. From this research, select organizations you feel will provide the best information.

Second:

* Locate a contact person in each organization who has the job or position you want to know about. It's also useful to talk with the CEO or even the board chairperson.

Third:

* Make the contact; pick up the phone and make the call. The first call is always the hardest. I've had clients who have resisted

making it. But, once you've succeeded, it's easy to continue. In fact, I've had clients get carried away with scheduling information interviews that I've had to urge them to begin analyzing the data and making decisions.

Fourth:

- Set a date and time for the interview. Be sure you have the correct name and spelling, title, address, location, etc., before you hang up.

- Immediately send a confirmation note stating the date and time; restate the purpose and objectives of your visit. Thank them for agreeing to meet.

Fifth:

- After the interview, immediately send a thank– you note. Highlight one or two of the important points you learned during the discussion. Say you'll follow up with the people they suggested you contact. And tell them you'll let them know what you eventually decide to do.

NOTES

NOTES

Key Point

• Be specific about your goal.

Here's a **sample telephone script** for setting up an information interview. Change it to fit your circumstances:

"Hello, my name is_____." (If someone recommended you to the contact, then say) *"_____ recommended that I talk with you."*

*"I'm making a career decision. In reflecting on my skills, experience, abilities, interests and talents, I'm focusing on _____ (occupa-*tion such as nursing, group practice administra-tion, etc.) *and particularly _____.* (Administrator, Controller, Director of Managed care). *As someone in this type of work, I would like to meet with you for no more than 30 minutes and ask some questions about the nature of your work, how you got started in it, what you think the future is for this kind of work, what you like or don't like about the work, and the type of experience or back-ground needed to be successful."*

"This information will help me in deciding whether to pursue _____ (the occupation/job) and, if so, what I must do to eventually become employed"

Here's a **sample thank–you note** to send someone after an interview. Adjust to your needs.

Dear Ms./Mr. _____ :
I appreciated the courtesy you extended to me in our meeting earlier this week. Considering the time demands on your schedule, it was very thoughtful. I was particularly interested to learn that _____ (relate one or two points you learned from the interview).

This information will help me make an informed decision about how I'd like to see my career progress. Some of what you described seems like a good match to my career goals. I will take your valuable advice and more forward.

Thank you for suggesting two colleagues I might talk with.

Again, thanks for your time.

Sincerely,

NOTES

Finding resources to help you prepare for information interviews

Here's a few selected resources that will help you prepare for information interviews. If your local library doesn't have them, try your local community college – its library or career center most likely will.

The Dictionary of Occupational Titles. Washington DC: US Government Printing Office. This publication describes, in some detail, what the career you're considering involves – what people in the field actually do. It also provides an idea of the skill level you need to be successful.

The Occupational Outlook Hand-book. New York: Rosen Publishing Group. Nicely overviews fields of interest. It provides general information about what people in the field do and earn, as well as the demand outlook, but doesn't list all careers.

The American Almanac of Jobs and Salaries, by John Wright. New York: Avon Books. This publication is printed biennially and lists job descriptions and annual earning information. It's a detailed and comprehensive listing of hundreds of occupations in a wide variety of industries and professions.

The Encyclopedia of Second Careers, by Gene R. Hawes. New York: Facts on file, 1984. This resource includes information similar to the *Occupational Outlook Hand– book.* It has excellent information on relating past experience to new career ideas. It's a good place to start if you're changing careers.

Your library has many other resources. Ask your librarian for help and explore!

Forming questions for information interviews

Here's a list of research questions you may want to use or adapt for your information interviews. The responses you receive will help you make decisions about your career.

- What are the major objectives of your position? What are you paid to accomplish?

- What do you do? What is a typical day like for you?

- What do you like about your work? What do you dislike?

- How did you get your start in this business? With this company?

- How did you get into this line of work? How did you learn to do what you do?

- What skills do you rely on most? Why?

- What are the typical working conditions? (e.g., environment, independence, travel)
- Whom do people in this field serve daily?

- What are the most difficult problems and decisions you face?

- Whom do you supervise? To whom do you report?

- How much variety is there in your work? How much specialization? How much routine?

- Are any degrees or licenses required?

- What kind of training, outside of degrees, is required? Why?

- What other credentials enhance a person's credibility in this field or position? Why?

- What is a typical starting salary? Intermediate or average level? Top levels?

- What is the range of compensation (salary, benefits, vacation, continuing education, etc.) a person can expect from this type of work in 5 to 6 years?

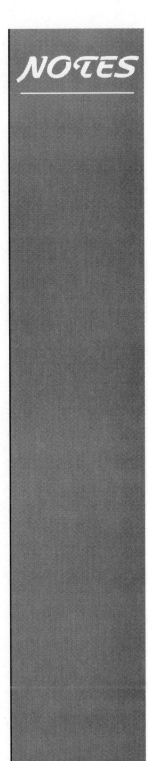

NOTES

- Where do you predict this line of work will be in 3 years? 5 years?

- Who are some of the leading organizations and individuals in this field?

- What is the current (future) market demand for people in this career (or job)? What are the prospects for the future?

- What hours do professionals in this field usually work? Is it common to bring work home?

- What personal or family sacrifices do people in this field make?

- What are some of the opportunities you anticipate over the next year in this field?

- If you leave this job, where could or would you go?

- How secure is employment in this field?

- What are the key skills needed to do this job well?

- What are the personality traits needed to be effective at this job?

- Looking back, if you had it to do over again, is there anything you would do differently?

- Who else does this type of work (or related occupation in which you are interested)? Who is successful and why?

- I would like to talk with (whoever was mentioned above). May I use your name in contacting him/her?

- What do you enjoy most about your profession?

- What separates you and your organization from the competition?

- What advice would you give someone just getting in the business?

- What one thing would you do with your business if you knew you couldn't fail?

- What significant changes have you seen take place in your profession through the years?

- What do you see as the coming trends in your business?

- What is the strangest or funniest incident you've experienced in your business?

- What ways have you found to be the most effective for promoting your business?

- What one sentence would you like people to use in describing the way you and your organization do business?

- What does it take to get to the top in this field?

Finally, the most important question to conclude the information interview:

- Who else would you suggest I contact?

  Or

- What other colleagues would you suggest I talk with?

What do I do with the information once I've completed my information interviews?

Use the information to help make decisions. For example, say your goal was to relocate to a different part of the country, but you don't know how managed care was affecting health care organizations in that area. Interviews with professionals from that part of the country would provide that information.

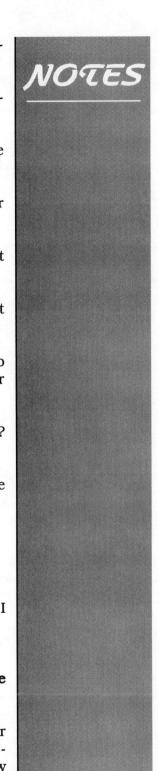

NOTES

In another situation, say your career goal was to get a financial analyst job in a major metropolitan hospital, but your experience included eight years managing a mid– size medical group practice. By interviewing professionals working as financial analysts in a hospital, you would get a better understanding of the required competencies and skills. You could then decide how your existing skills transfer to a hospital environment and how best to present your skills in an interview.

Information interviews provide needed data which will help you make more informed career decisions.

Job interviews

Job interviews are usually with the person who has the authority to hire you; it could be the person to whom you would report. These interviews take place as a result of your: 1) customizing your cover letter and resume in response to a classified ad in the newspaper or in a trade journal; 2) passing a screening interview; or 3) uncovering a job lead through networking.

During a job interview, interviewers always ask questions to determine whether your qualifications, experience and background match the job requirements. More important, they're determining if you will fit the organization – asking themselves "Can I work with you and will you successfully work with our team?"

At the same time, *you're interviewing the organization* to determine whether it will fit your goals. Does the position and its growth potential align with your career goals and objectives? Does the culture match your preferences?

Typically the format for job interviews is one person at a time, but group or committee interviews are becoming more popular. More on this later.

Prepare for the first job interview

You're anxious, maybe a little nervous. All your hard work has led to this outcome – a face-to-face job interview. Finally, an opportunity; you want to put your best foot forward and make a positive impression. How should you prepare?

Heed three important tips when preparing for the interview

1. Never assume the interviewer is prepared to interview you. Anticipate the interviewer won't be prepared and, in fact, may have thought about the interview only minutes before you arrived. Interviewers typically think of and ask questions off the top of their heads. They may be as uncomfortable and tense as you are.

2. Don't assume the interviewer will take sole responsibility for the interview. You must prepare yourself to participate, even guide, the interview in order to find out as much information as you can about the job and the employer's needs. Once you have identified job responsibilities and needs, you can discuss your skills and accomplishments in terms of those needs. Employers want to find solutions to their problems. Your skills must offer that solution.

3. Remember that interviewers evaluate and decide about you based on not only your knowledge and skills but also your:

   • Accomplishments and achievements;
   • Career and job goals;
   • Communication and relationship skills;
   • Ability to "fit" into the organization;
   • Appearance; and
   • Overall impression.

Thus, you must be ready to control or, at least, direct the flow of the interview. Your ultimate goal continues as it has been in the past – matching your experiences and skills to the requirements of the job. Even though the interviewer has reviewed your resume and decided to interview you based on it, consider the interview your first chance to sell yourself – face-to-face. Approach the interview as if the interviewer knew nothing about you or your background.

To take advantage of these tips, keep in mind that your goal for the first interview is to get a second interview. Given this objective and the notion that most interviewers aren't well prepared, here's how to take control of the interview:

- Review the guidelines for results-oriented interviewing;
- Plan for trait and behavior questions;
- Know and plan for common interview questions, including ones designed to screen you out;
- Know the questions asked entry-level candidates;
- Have some questions of your own ready;
- Survive the critical first 30 seconds and build rapport;
- Prepare and use your 2-1/2-minute drill (discussed later in this chapter);
- Listen and interact with interviewers in a positive way;
- Ask questions to uncover needs and requirements;
- Describe your accomplishments; tell stories that directly relate to their needs and requirements;
- Conclude the interview in a positive way – summarize;
- Identify next steps; and
- Send a follow-up letter.

Let's talk about each of these control steps in more detail.

Guidelines for results-oriented interviewing

These guidelines should help set the stage for a successful interview. First, keep these ideas in mind:

- A successful outcome for the first interview is to get the second face-to-face interview – NOT to get a job offer. That will come later;

- During any interview your job is to uncover needs, problems and issues. Then show how your skills and accomplishments match up against those needs; and

- The interviewers' objective is to "screen you out of consideration" during the interview, NOT to look for the reasons they should hire you.

Now, focus on four key aspects of interviewing: your presentation, preparation, listening skills and responses.

Your presentation

1. Remember first impressions. You make a significant impression on the interviewer during the first 30 seconds.

2. Convey impressions that often lead interviewers to reach subconscious conclusions – even before you speak.

3. Be yourself; just be your BEST self.

Your preparation

1. Plan your drive time to arrive early – at least 30 minutes early. Waiting in the parking lot is better than getting stuck in traffic.

2. Dress consistently with the organization's and position's culture; be conservative.

3. Plan your attitude – positive attitude and body posture.

4. Talk about your skills and accomplishments and how they match the needs of the organization.

5. Anticipate the most often asked question: "Tell me about yourself."

6. Think of the interview as an exchange of information between two people. Answer each question with brief statements – don't use more than 90 to 100 seconds for each response.

Listening skills

1. Prepare and be confident in your own material and presentation so you can actively attend (listen) to the interviewer.

2. Listen for clues in what the interviewer says and in the voice inflection. Respond to those clues. Also look for clues in their non–verbal cues.

3. Paraphrase what is said as a way of confirming what you've heard.

4. Prepare 5 to 10 questions, but remember, you may use only three or four.

Your responses

1. Always respond positively and energetically.

2. Never talk negatively about previous employers, no matter how bad the situation was.

3. Focus all your responses on the job and the employer's needs, not on your needs and requests.

4. Resist the urge to suggest solutions to problems discussed. Suggest how your experience makes it likely that you will help solve problems.

5. Don't reject anything before it is offered or let negative reactions show. Keep an open mind; you can always say "no" later.

6. Send a thank-you note immediately after the interview. Prepare a separate thank-you note for the secretary or administrative assistant.

Plan for trait and behavioral questions

Two types of interview questions are typical. One focuses on your traits; the other explores your behavior.

Trait questions

Sometimes referred to as personality interviews, trait questions are a structured way to assess your personality traits – organizational skills, flexibility, adaptability, energy and motivation, just to name a few. Trait questions relate more to characteristics of your personality than to your job skills.

Before each interview, identify personality traits that best describe the things you do well in relation to the job's requirements. Have the words ready when describing yourself. Use the following questions to help you prepare for trait-related questions you *will* be asked.

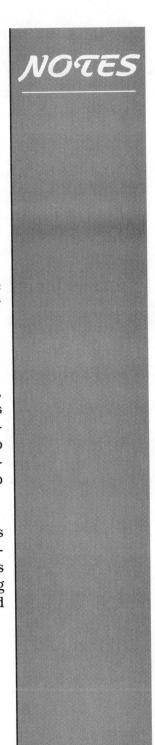

NOTES

223

Question: What are your two most positive qualities? Why?

Your response: _____
                    _____
                    _____

Question: How creative are you?

Your response: _____
                    _____
                    _____

Question: How would you describe your flexibility or adaptability?

Your response: _____
                    _____
                    _____

Question: To what extent are you an organized person?

Your response: _____
                    _____
                    _____

Now think of other questions like these and write down your responses to them. The more you practice, the less likely such questions will surprise you in the interview.

Behavior–based questions

In behavior-based interviews, you are asked open–ended questions to encourage you to describe a past action or achievement – how you handled a particular problem or a difficult person. For example, an interviewer wanting to know how you handle difficult people in a public setting may ask:

"Tell me about a time when you were able to satisfy an irate customer."

The phrase "a time when . . ." prompts you to think of a specific example from your experience and describe what you did, how you acted, and the result. General responses, such as "I always get along with customers," won't be satisfactory. The behavioral-based interview is designed to get behind the generalities and examine specific behaviors, actions and results.

NOTES

Use the following questions to help you prepare for behavior-based questions you *will* be asked.

Question: "Tell me about a time when you had to organize a project at work. What did you do?"

Your response: _____

                          _____

                          _____

Question: "Describe a time when you had to persuade a coworker to agree with your point of view. What did you do?"

Your response: _____

                          _____

                          _____

Question: "Think of a time when you had adapt to a change you didn't like or agree with. What did you do?"

Your response: _____

                          _____

                          _____

Question: "Tell me about a time you disagreed with your boss. How did you handle it? How did it turn out?"

Your response: _____

                          _____

                          _____

Question: "Think of a time when your interpersonal skills were needed to solve a sticky employee problem. How did you handle the situation? What was the outcome?"

Your response: _____

                          _____

                          _____

Question: "Do you remember having resolved a conflict among team members? What did you do?"

Your response: _____
                 _____
                 _____

Question: "Describe a time when you were motivated to complete a project. Why were you motivated?"

Your response: _____
                 _____
                 _____

Question: "Tell me about a time when you lacked the motivation to follow through on an assignment or project. How did you handle it?"

Your response: _____
                 _____
                 _____

Question: "Describe a project you managed that was loaded with problems and obstacles. What did you do?"

Your response: _____
                 _____
                 _____

Question: "Describe a time when your job requirements changed. How did you react? How did you handle it?"

Your response: _____
                 _____
                 _____

Question: "How do you relate work projects to your career goals?"

Your response: _____
                 _____
                 _____

Know and plan for common interview questions – using your resume database

Following are sample questions often asked during a first job interview. You must prepare to respond to these and others like them. Do so by reviewing your resume database (refer to Chapter 3). Then focus your preparation on achievements and accomplishments you believe closely match the organization's needs. Also, notice how the questions focus on either behaviors, traits or your character. Interviewers are looking for any indication as to how your past behavior (experience) is a match and if your traits (personality characteristics) and character (moral qualities) are consistent with the organization's culture and staff.

Remember, the information you provide on these questions helps the employer explore your present and past work history, what you've accomplished, and how you handled certain situations or solved problems.

I've organized the sample questions into five general areas:

1) Questions designed to screen you out;

2) Other questions common to first interviews arranged into three categories:

   • Professional experience;
   • Managing and supervising experience; and
   • Personal background.

3) Two questions often used to end the first interview;

4) Questions sometimes used for entry– level positions; and

5) Questions you should have ready to ask during the interview.

Learn the questions designed to screen you out

These are the tough questions. Their intent is to find something wrong with you – in the interviewer's mind. The best way to answer these probing questions is to be brief and positive. This is not easy because of how the interviewer may "perceive" your response. Perceptions are not necessarily the truth – it's how the interviewer interprets your response. You must strive to respond in a way that changes a potential negative interpretation into a positive.

Here are examples of typical "screen out" questions you'll face during interviews. I've provided a short explanation as to why each could screen you out.

1.   What are your weaknesses and strengths?

The screen out: A perceived job related weakness by the interviewer. For example, I had a client who was one of three final job candidates. During her third interview, she was asked to describe a weakness. She said she needed to develop skills in using spread-sheet software. The other two candidates had these skills. The result: my client was eliminated from consideration. This was unfortunate because my client could have quickly improved her skills without affecting overall job performance.

Your response to "strengths" can have the same effect. When responding, be sure you are describing a strength that is valued by the interviewer and the organization, and that address a need or job requirement.

2.   What are your salary requirements?

The screen out: If you state a salary requirement that's too high, you may be perceived as "too expensive or experienced." If you indicate a salary that's too low, you may be perceived as "too inexperienced or lacking self–worth." In each case, you may be eliminated early in the hiring process.

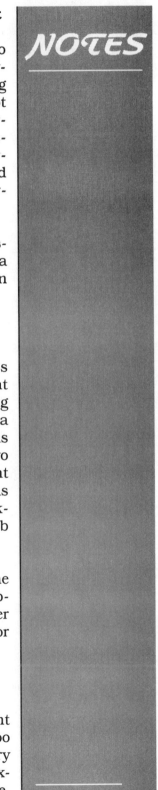

NOTES

229

Beware! This question can surface in many different ways. For example, interviewers may use questions like:

- What's your current salary?;
- What salary were you earning before?;
- What's your current compensation package?;
- What do you think a job like this should pay?;
- Describe your previous salary increases;
- What was the percentage of your last increase? Was it what you were expecting?; or
- What do you feel was a fair increase? What was it to be based on?

The general screen out rule-of-thumb applies in each case. Always be alert to and respond accordingly to salary-related questions.

3. Did your group have a formal process for performance reviews? How was it used?

The screen out: The interviewer may believe you are hiding a past performance problem. Lack of a formal review process could be interrupted in a way that questions your employment record – it may not be as good, or as complete, as you are describing.

4. How did you like your last job?

The screen out: The interviewer is searching for clues that might indicate relationship or attitude problems that might affect your performance. Your response must be positive, for example:

"My last job provided the opportunity to learn and use many different skills. For example, I was able to . . . ."

5. How did you get along with your former boss?

The screen out: As before, the interviewer is searching for clues that might indicate relationship or attitude problems. Put a positive spin on your response. Never leave the impression that you couldn't get along or communicate with your boss. For example:

"My boss was very good at making sure I had the opportunity to work on a variety of challenging projects. I've always had a good relationship with my employer."

6. Tell me about your greatest disappointment in your life?

The screen out: The interviewer is searching for how you handled the disappointment – did you face the situation head–on or did you run from it. Focus your response on how you learned and grew from the experience. For example:

"Everyone has disappointments. I always look at them as an opportunity to learn and grow from the experience. Here's an example . . . ."

7. Doesn't this job represent a career switch for you?

The screen out: The interviewer may not be convinced you have the skills to do the job. A possible response is:

"Not really. I'll use the same skills and abilities . . . . "

Then give an example of how your skills connect between your past (or current) job and the one for which you are being interviewed.

231

NOTES

8. Why did you leave your last job?

The screen out: Were you downsized from your last job and, if so, what were the reasons. Be specific when you give reasons for leaving your last job. For example, if you were caught in a lay-off because of a merger then say:

> *"Because of an integration (merger or affiliation) with another group, my job was eliminated. This has given me the opportunity to explore several different exciting options. This is why this position appealed to me."*

9. (If you are a women) Do you plan to have children? Get married?

The screen out: This, or course, is an illegal question, but don't get overly concerned. The employer is interested only in exploring possible future problem areas such as time away from the job or an extended leave of absence. Respond calmly.

Let's think about the purpose of questions like these and the effect your responses could have on the outcome of the interview. First, a rule of thumb:

> Always respond to a "negatively" focused question with a positive.

For example, how would you respond to this question? *"Tell me about one of your weaknesses."*

One possible response:

> *"If I'm working with a project team and I see a team member who isn't as committed as I am, I sometimes get upset about it. I know I shouldn't expect every team member to be as committed as I am. That is something I'm working on."*

Here's why this response works: you've changed "weakness" into a personality trait that shows you're committed to work and hold people to high standards.

Here's another possible response that can be fun to use but only if you and the interviewer have developed a rapport.

"Chocolate. I'm a chocoholic."

Usually, this type of response is well accepted. Once the moment is over, though, you ask a more focused question of the interviewer to get away from the weakness question.

Some of the questions listed previously are illegal. If you feel they are too personal, say so, and ask the interviewer to move on to another question. Be careful – some interviewers are very skillful at asking illegal questions by making them seem like they're not even questions.

For example, let's suppose a female is interviewing for a position in another city, so accepting an offer would mean relocation. A question interviewers may want to ask but know they can't legally is – *"Are you married?"* . The issue is, of course, that if she is married, her husband would also have to find work. A sneaky way to find out this information is for the interviewer to ask a question like *"What does your husband do for a living?"* A question like this may even come up over lunch or on the way to or from the airport. Seems innocent enough, and most times an honest response is fine. Just be aware that your response could be taken many ways.

You could discuss the type of work your husband does and the interviewer could figure it may be difficult to find him work, so they may not make an offer. Or, suppose you're single, and you respond, "Oh, I'm not married." Your marital status could be positive or a negative.

Being married could be interpreted as being settled down and more dependable – a positive; it could mean

NOTES

233

having to help find your husband a job – a possible negative. Being married may imply that you have children, meaning child–care issues and time away from work – a negative. But the group could be a family–oriented practice that expects children – a positive.

Being single could be interpreted as having flexibility, able to accept out–of–town projects – a positive. But it could be seen as being unsettled and unpredictable – a negative. I've consulted with single clients who have heard they weren't hired because the job required travel with other company staff who were married, and the organization didn't want married staff traveling with single staff of the opposite sex. Discrimination – yes. Could this person do anything? Not really.

Learn other common questions.

Most other interview questions ask about your professional experience, managing and supervising experience or personal background.

On professional experience

1. Tell me (us) about yourself.

2. How did you decide to work for your current (or most recent) organization?

3. What are the objectives and responsibilities of your current job?

4. What are your functional responsibilities?

5. What parts of this job do you enjoy the most? The least? Why?

6. What size budget do you manage in your current (or most recent) job?

7. Describe one (or two) recent successes you've had in accomplishing an objective or goal. What did you do?

8. Describe two or three recent major accomplishments. Why are they important to you?

9. What was the impact of these accomplishments on the organization?

10. Tell me about a situation in which you increased profits? Decreased costs?

11. What do you consider the most important idea you contributed? Your most interesting achievement? Why?

12. Describe a recent failure you had. How did you react and handle it? What were the outcomes?

13. What steps have you taken to improve your performance in that area(s)?

14. Describe one or two of the major challenges or problems now affecting your group? What is your role in handling these issues?

15. Tell me about how you like to make decisions.

16. What was the most important policy decision you have made?

17. When you are under pressure to meet a deadline or complete a task, how do you get the people around you to help?

18. Tell me about the kinds of risks you've taken in the past.

19. Describe your current boss or supervisor. What adjectives would best describe her or him? Why?

20. What are the positive characteristics you look for in a supervisor?

21. What management style do you prefer in a boss?

22. What have you learned from your current (or most recent) boss?

23. In which areas is (was) your boss most likely to give you positive feedback? Explain.

24. In which areas is (was) your boss the most critical? Why?

25. If you didn't agree with the criticism, how did you handle it? What did you do? What was the outcome?

26. Tell me about a time you and your boss disagreed on an important issue. How did you handle the situation? What was the outcome?

27. How well do you work with project teams? Tell me about a time when you felt you weren't productive in a team setting. Why weren't you productive? How did you handle it?

28. How do you handle conflict between peers? Describe a time when you've had to solve a conflict with a peer. People you supervise? Your boss?

29. Tell me about a time when you had to settle a dispute between physician owners of the group. How did you handle the situation?

30. Are you creative? Describe a specific situation.

31. In which of the various environments you have worked were you most productive? Least productive? Why?

32. Which of your previous positions has best prepared you for this job? Why?

33. What are you greatest technical strengths? Describe.

34. In what technical areas do you think you need more development to become proficient?

35. What do you know about our organization or group?

36. Why do you feel you are qualified for this job?

37. What do you have to offer us?

38. When have you enjoyed your job the most? The least?

39. With your experience, why aren't you in a higher-level position?

40. What unusual skills do you have that others might not be able to offer us?

41. It seems as though you are over-qualified (under-qualified) for this position. Why are you interested?

42. How long would you plan to stay with our organization?

43. How satisfied do you feel you would be after working 12 months in this position? Why?

44. Given what you know about this job, how long do you feel it would take you to make a contribution here?

45. Are you qualified for this job? Why?

46. What qualifications do you bring to the job?

47. With which aspects of the position do you feel most comfortable? Least comfortable?

48. Do you feel you lack any qualifications for this job? Is this critical? Why? Why not?

49. What would be one of the first things you would do in this position? Why?

50. What will your references say about you?

51. If you were me, would you hire you for this position? Why?

52. What are your career aspirations?

53. If you could begin your career again, what would you do differently?

54. Whom do you admire as a leader in American history? Why?

55. Are you interviewing with any other organization?

56. Does your employer know you are job hunting? Why or why not?

57. Why do you have time gaps in your resume?

58. What questions do you have for me (us)?

On managing and supervising

59. Describe your management (leadership) philosophy. Management style.

60. What do you think is the difference between leadership and management? Why?

61. How would you describe effective management (leadership)?

62. What are the characteristics of bad management (leadership)?

63. What specific techniques do you use to manage people? How have they worked for you in the past? Discuss.

64. How do you encourage staff freedom and participation in organization decisions/ problem– solving?

65. What kinds of decisions do you typically delegate to others? Not delegate? Why?

66. What criteria do you use to measure staff performance?

67. How would your past direct reports describe your management style?

68. What are your managing or supervising strengths? Weaknesses? Why?

69. What would others say you could improve upon? Why?

70. What do you look for when hiring people?

71. Tell me about the people you have hired. How long did they stay with you?

72. When did you last fire someone? What were the circumstances? How did you react?

73. How many people do you manage or supervise? How many non-exempt? Exempt?

74. How do you motivate staff? What is a specific example in which you successfully motivated someone? What did you do?

75. How do you reward positive performance? Any techniques you feel work better than others?

76. How do you handle poor or marginal performance? Describe a specific example.

77. What are your beliefs about training and professional development for you and your staff?

78. How effective are you in planning? Why?

79. Typically, how do you establish goals and objectives with direct reports?

80. How do you monitor progress?

81. What would you consider to be your greatest strengths as a manager? Why?

On personal matters

82. Describe yourself. What adjectives would you use? Why?

83. If I were to talk to the people you have worked for, what would they be likely to say about you?

84 How would your peers, direct reports or boss describe you? What adjectives would they use?

85. How do you start a day?

86. How do you like to spend your free time? What are your hobbies?
87. Are you active in the community?

88. How have you personally invested in your professional or personal development?

89. In what ways have you tried to improve yourself?

90. What are your greatest strengths or attributes? Why?

91. If you could change something about yourself, what would it be? Why?

92. What are your goals in life?

93. What are your career goals? How does this position fit in?

94 What are you looking for in a career? A job?

95. How would you describe your personality?

96. What caused you to leave your last position?

97. Why are you interested in this job?

98. How would you describe your ideal job environment? Why is this important to you?

99. When have you found your career most enjoyable? Least enjoyable?

100. Describe your personality type. Knowing what you do about us, how do you see your personality type matching with our culture?

101. Generally, how do you feel about yourself?

102. How is your health?

Plan your responses to typical concluding questions.

104. Do you have any other questions of us?

105. Is there anything else you want to know about us or you feel is important we know about you?

Always respond to these two questions.

First example:

"Do you have any other questions of us?"

Response: "Yes, I do. Just let me scan the list of questions I brought to see which ones we haven't answered. Here's one . . . . "

If no questions are unanswered, always think of one or two on-the-spot. Never say you don't have other questions.

Second example:

"Is there anything else you want to know about us or you feel is important we know about you?"

Response: "Yes. I'd like to summarize two of my qualifications that I believe are a strong match to what you're looking for. First . . . ."

Always respond to this question by restating one or two areas in which your qualifications closely match the requirements or needs of the job.

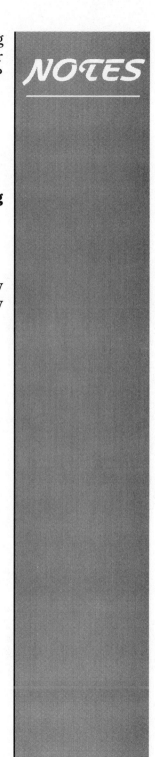

241

Know the questions asked entry–level candidates

If you're new to health management, you won't have the job experience of a seasoned candidate, so interviewers will focus on how your school and other experiences qualify you for their entry-level position. Here are some typical questions:

1. Which university or college did you attend?

2. How did you select that particular one?

3. Which other schools did you consider? Why were they eliminated?

4. Why did you decide to attend graduate school?

5. When did you decide to major in health care administration? What led you to that decision?

6. If you could repeat your college education again, would you choose a different major? Why? Why not?

7. Describe the kind of student you were. What adjectives would you use? Why?

8. Which subjects or courses did you like the best? The least? Why?

9. Did you participate in any extracurricular activities? Describe.

10. What leadership role did you play in any of these activities?

11. Did you work part– or full–time during school? How did those experiences prepare you for work in health care?

12. How do you feel your college (undergraduate or graduate) education prepared you for this position? For working in general?

13. Did you write a thesis? If so, what was its focus or objective?

14. How did you like doing the research? What did you like or dislike about it?

Have some of your own questions ready.

Always have five questions ready to ask the interviewer, even though you use only two or three. Every interviewer may not evaluate you on the questions you ask, BUT they will evaluate you negatively if you don't have questions. Why? Because they expect you to be interested enough in their organization and culture to match your abilities to their needs. Otherwise, you're taking no responsibility for the "goodness of fit" between you and the position. Here are some typical questions you may want to ask:

1. Tell me about the major duties and responsibilities of this position.

2. What are the organization's short– and long–range plans?

3. How does this job fit in with those plans and objectives?

4. What are your critical objectives for this year? Next year?

5. Why is this position open? Is it a new position?

6. What happened to the last person who had this job?

7. What have been the main reasons people have had for leaving this job?

8. What would you like to do more (or less) of next year?

9. What does your organization pride itself on?

Handle the first job interview – take charge

Survive the critical first 30 seconds and build rapport

Here's an interesting fact: within the first 30 seconds of meeting you, interviewers won't know whether they will eventually offer you the job, BUT they WILL know if they WON'T hire you. First impressions are critical to your success. Practice and be confident how you communicate to others by controlling your posture, expression, your first statements, firmness of your hand shake, moistness of your hands, and eye contact. These all affect that critical first impression.

In addition, pay attention to the surroundings – the environment – for clues that will help during the interview. Is the working environment open, bright, colorful? Do other staff seem to be having fun? Do people smile? Does the environment seem strictly business, with few personal items on walls or desks? Are people talking with each other, or do they seem to keep to themselves? Use your observations to decide how you want to conduct the interview: business-like, interspersed with lightness and fun, or strictly business?

Use small talk to your benefit

Use travel time to the meeting room to your advantage. Engage in small talk to help break the ice and to begin building rapport. Keep it short though – no more than four to five minutes. If the interview is to be in an executive's office, look for personal items that suggest personality. These observations may help you focus your small talk.

I interviewed with a medical director of a major HMO for a consulting contract. On his office wall was a collage of what appeared to be his children – all 17 of them. That's right, 17 kids. Here was an obvious conversation point. Turned out he and his wife were foster parents of these 17 kids. Our short discussion proved to be a very positive way to break the ice for the discussion yet to come.

Establish the time allowed for the interview

The next step on your "greeting" agenda is to find out how much time has been set aside for the interview. You must find out about any time constraints to plan your time accordingly. Knowing how long you have is critical because you want time to ask all the questions you need to ask. You don't want to run out of time.

Begin the interview forcefully

Take charge of the interview at this point. Plan your transition from small-talk to beginning the interview. Rather than waiting for the interviewer to transition into the interview itself, I suggest you begin by saying:

"Perhaps a good place for us to begin is if I tell you a little bit about myself."

This is an excellent statement you can use to begin your 2-1/2-minute drill, which is your response to the question most often asked first:

"Tell me about yourself."

Read on to learn about this drill.

NOTES

Prepare and use a 2-1/2-minute drill

The 2-1/2-minute presentation is a speech you have prepared before the interview. In 2-1/2-minutes – no longer – you synopsize yourself and your professional history to match the interviewer's needs and situation. You also want to present information in a way that motivates the interviewer to ask more questions – to want to hear more about you and your background. This technique:

1. Helps put you and the interviewer at ease.
2. Helps you take charge of the interview.

A visual of the process is on the next page.

The 2-1/2-minute speech step-by-step process

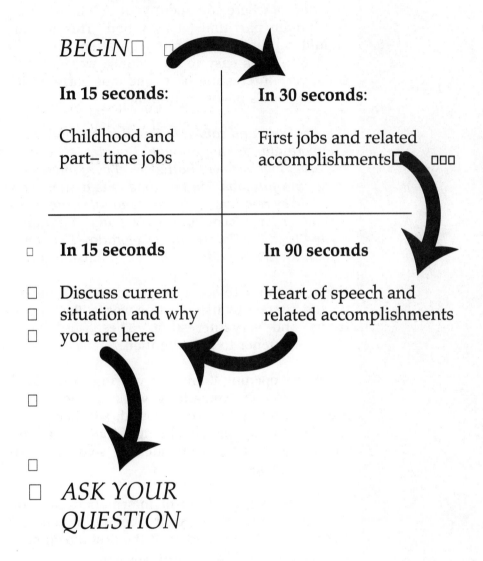

BEGIN

In 15 seconds:

Childhood and
part– time jobs

In 30 seconds:

First jobs and related
accomplishments

In 15 seconds

Discuss current
situation and why
you are here

In 90 seconds

Heart of speech and
related accomplishments

*ASK YOUR
QUESTION*

Let's review each of the five parts of your 2-1/2-minute drill.

Part 1: Getting started – 15 seconds

Begin your 2– 1/2–minute speech with an overview of where you spent your childhood (grew up) and any part-time jobs you had. This opening should capture the interviewer's attention. For most of us, it's easy to do because we've all had some very interesting part-time jobs early in our career. Here's how I begin mine:

> *I was born and raised in Boulder and had the opportunity to go through Boulder schools. During high school I had several very interesting and fun jobs. My best one was a summer job delivering lumber in the mountains around Boulder for a local lumber company. I graduated from the University of Colorado – Boulder with an undergraduate degree in business.*

Notice in about 15 seconds, you can catch the listener's interest by using action words like "opportunity" and "very interesting." These words motivate the listener to pay attention.

I use this opening if I'm interviewing with a local organization for consulting work. I know there aren't too many "natives" around, so I like to use that fact for my benefit. Being a "native" catches the listener's ear and provides for some interesting discussion.

What interesting tidbits of information can you think of to include in your opening statement? Take a few minutes and draft the first fifteen minutes of your 2– 1/2– minute speech.

Part 2: First jobs – 30 seconds

In part 2, you describe one or two of your first jobs – those jobs right out of college. Include at least one related accomplishment statement. Continuing with my example:

After graduation from the University of Colorado I was fortunate to be offered my first full-time job with the Department of Continuing Education, the same department I had worked with during summer breaks. I was with this department for eight years during which time I got my graduate degree and became Assistant Director of Programs. This provided me with my first real-time work experience and was invaluable in helping me establish most of my work values and habits.

After completing graduate school, I went to work for the Farm Credit System as a program manager. It was at this job that my education really paid off for me. While with Farm Credit I . . . . (describe one or two major accomplishments that links to the needs of the interviewer).

Again, notice my use of the action or motivating words like "first real," "invaluable" and "really paid off." These words create interest with the listener. Continue drafting your speech. Write part 2.

Part 3: Body of speech – 90 seconds

This is the major section of your 2-1/2–minute drill. During this 90 seconds you describe two or three accomplishments that closely match the interviewer's requirements. It will pay dividends to think about each interview opportunity and customize what you want to say.

Continue drafting your speech. Include two or three accomplishments but recognize you may substitute others depending on the interview.

Part 4: Current situation – 15 seconds

Here you answer one important question BEFORE interviewers ask it. This is your chance to describe your situation and explain why you are interviewing here. Assume that the interviewer is

NOTES

wondering why you applied for the position. Answer the question before it's asked. For example, if you've recently been downsized, then say:

"My group or organization went through an integration (merger, affiliation) and my job was eliminated during the change."

This is all you need to say at this point. You will probably have an opportunity to say more about the downsizing later in the interview.

Part 5: Directive question – 5 seconds

The LAST statement you make in your 2-1/2-minute drill:

"I've told you a little bit about me. Now, could you describe the job, the major responsibilities, and the key objectives or goals for the next year."

Without being too directive, this statement suggests the next steps of the interview – for the interviewer to describe the job and its major responsibilities. This helps in three ways: 1) it cues interviewers that it's their turn to talk; 2) it focuses interviewers to talk about the job in an organized way; and 3) it allows you to listen to interviewers discuss the job. Once interviewers describe their needs, you can decide which accomplishment stories you want to respond with, thus continuing to direct the interview.

Don't forget to include this question in your speech.

I've heard about (and been part of) many interviews in which the interviewer is not well prepared and starts off with a barrage of unrelated questions. If the interviewer isn't focused, you aren't focused. Too many times the interviewer will begin with a question like *"Tell me what you can do"* or *"Tell me what you do (did) at your current job."* Then, what happens is the candidates go into depth about what they do, only to be told, *"That's all fine and good, but we don't need someone with that background. Thanks for coming in. Good-bye."*

At this point, as the candidate, you're lost. The interview is a bust. That's why I coach my clients to end their 2-1/2-minute drill with that all-important question.

By the way, draft your drill and then practice it several times to hone it down to 2-1/2 minutes. Once it's memorized, you can review it in your mind as you drive to an interview. You'll never say the same thing twice in a row. As long as you have the template of the speech memorized, you'll adapt what you say to the situation at hand. You may begin with your early childhood information, but in some cases, you may decide to begin at part 3 – recent accomplishments that apply to the job you are interviewing for.

Try it; keep it flexible but use it. It works!

The worksheet on the following page should help you begin drafting your speech.

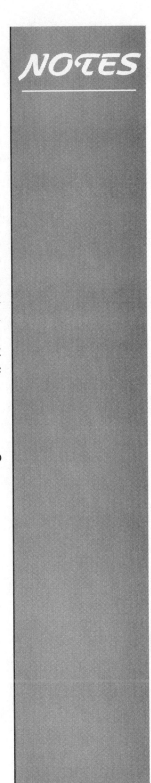

Worksheet for your 2-1/2-minute speech

Childhood, education, part-time jobs and interests
** 15 seconds **

Early adult life, first job, early accomplishment(s)
** 30 seconds **

What you do, career progress and growth, accomplishments
** 90 seconds **

Your current situation, recent change, "why you are here"
** 15 seconds**

Ask question about job requirements

Attend to interviews in a positive way

Your skills in non–verbal behavior affect how well you interview. To help you monitor and maintain your listening ability – attend. When you *"attend" to interviewers*, you give them your full attention by listening with your body and your mind. Make sure you face interviewers, giving them full eye contact. Attending during an interview takes discipline because you must put your questions and needs aside for the moment and give interviewers the stage. This can be difficult but, when done correctly, it will signal to interviewers your interest and receptivity to what they are saying.

Continually monitor your non–verbal behavior. For example, be aware of your posture – sit straight and tall in the chair; don't slouch. Sit so you have direct eye contact – so you won't have distractions such as a window or a hallway with lots of activity.

Acknowledge the interviewer's message, by leaning slightly forward and responding with statements like:

- "That sounds like an exciting and interesting project";

- "I can tell this position is critical to helping the practice accomplish its overall goals";

- "That idea is really exciting. Tell me more about it."; or

- "What else can you tell me about that project?"

Statements like these communicate to interviewers – verbally and non-verbally – that you're interested in what they are describing.

Take notes while listening. Early in the interview, tell the interviewer that you will be taking notes. Interviewers are impressed by people who take notes. Don't try to write everything the interviewer says. Capture themes of what the interviewer is

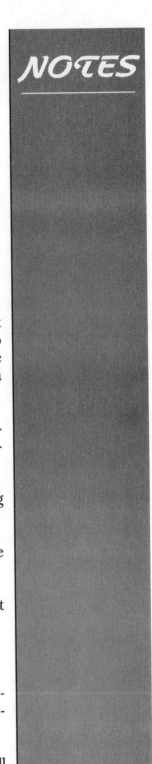

describing by using short phrases that summarize those main points. For example, when the interviewer is describing the critical duties of the job, you could summarize by listing key words like managed care-contracting, budgeting, negotiating with vendors, capitation, new policy manual, etc. You can add detail when you review your notes after the interview.

Try attending and taking notes the next time you're in an interview. These are difficult skills to master, but once you do, you'll be much more effective.

Ask questions to uncover needs and requirements

As you listen to the needs and requirements an interviewer describes, form your own open-ended questions. Open-ended questions help you gather or fill in missing information. Use questions that begin with who, what, where, when, and how. Avoid Why questions – they can be interpreted as challenging, blaming, or calling on someone to justify or defend a position. Open-ended questions encourage interviewers to explain in greater detail, expand discussion on a certain topic, or explore an issue in more depth.

Avoid using closed questions because they usually curtail discussion rather than expand it, often resulting in a "yes" or "no" response. In an interview, you're trying to encourage interviewers to expand the discussion, not shorten it. Beware of using closed questions as if they were open-ended. Examples: "Would you like to tell me more about that project?" or "Do you know if there will be any problems doing that?" The answer to either question could easily be a "yes" or "no" – a response that doesn't help you explore issues.

Describe your accomplishments; tell stories that directly relate to interviewer needs and requirements

Remember those accomplishment statements that took you so long to write for your resume database in Chapter 3? You used them in your resume and in your cover letters; now you will use them during the interview.

As you listen to the interviewer describe the major responsibilities of the job (you *are* actively listening, right?), you're also pulling from your resources, the accomplishments you want to use to describe your experience. Think of accomplishment statements as stories you'll use to show what you did and what came of each activity. The more research you do before the interview, the better you'll be able to pre-select these accomplishment statements.

This technique to successful interviewing is what makes interviewing so difficult. At the same time you're actively listening (and attending) to the interviewer, you're also forming a response by selecting which accomplishment stories you want to use. Preparation and practice using the techniques we've discussed in this chapter will help you succeed.

Conclude the interview in a positive way – summarize

Leave enough time at the end of an interview to summarize the discussion. This is your last chance to "remind" interviewers about areas in which your skills most closely match their needs. Refer to notes you've taken during the interview – those major themes you've written down.

Identify next steps

In your continuing effort to take charge of your job search, conclude the interview by suggesting the next steps *you'll* take.

Here's what typically happens. A candidate asks what the next steps are, and interviewers say, *"We still have several candidates to interview. After the interviews are finished, we'll make our decision and get back with you, probably in a week or so."* The candidate politely says, *"Okay, I look forward to hearing from you."* And, that's it. As a result, one week and then maybe two weeks go by. The candidate still hasn't heard anything, begins to wonder what happened, and doesn't know if he or she should call.

Here's what I recommend. At the end of your interview ask about the next steps, but follow up by suggesting you'll call in _____x_____ days to discuss those steps. In other words, give yourself permission to call – at a predetermined time and date.

Send a follow–up letter

Here's another critical step. Make sure you follow your interview with a short but pointed thank–you note. Take a few minutes when you get to your car and note a few things said during the interview that you felt went well. Immediately prepare and send a note highlighting those two or three areas in which you believe your skills matched their requirements.

If you traveled to another city for the interview, take the time on the plane ride home to draft your follow-up letter. Put it in the mail the next day.

Here's another technique that works. If the interview was in your home town, **hand deliver** it the next day. Give it to a receptionist or secretary, **not** to the person who interviewed you. If you try to hand it directly to the interviewer, he or she may think you're trying to "get extra attention" or "extend your interview opportunity."

Here's a sample follow-up letter, from Chapter 5:

Date

Dear Mr./Ms./Dr.:

Thanks again for the opportunity to meet and discuss your requirements for a clinic administrator.

The more I thought about our discussion, the more convinced I am about how well my previous experience with _____ and _____ matches three of your critical objectives for the coming year.

I'll call you June 23rd to follow–up our interview and see what our next steps might be.

In the meantime, please call if you have questions. My number is (111) 555 – 1212.

Cordially,

Take charge of your second and subsequent interviews

Congratulations! You've passed your first test and have been promoted to round two of the interview process. Now your work really begins – competing with one to ten candidates who all are potential matches and can do the job.

First interviews separate likely candidates from ones who simply don't fit the interviewer's criteria. In upcoming interviews, interviewers will probe for personal style, fit with colleagues and the organization, understanding of the job, and commitment to the organization's mission and goals. Interviewers will evaluate your potential to make a contribution to bottom-line results – what you can do for them rather than what you've done in the past.

There are different "rules" for the second and any subsequent interviews. Yes, you continue to match your skills to their needs, but, in addition, you should now focus on your needs. It's your opportunity to assess if:

•   their compensation package is appropriate;

•   this opportunity will help meet your career goal;

•   the working environment and colleagues match your personality; and

•   professional development and career advancement opportunities are available.

Key Point

• You are interviewing the organization

Remember, not only is the organization using these interviews to help decide if it wants to offer you the job, but you are also interviewing the organization – to help you decide if this is an organization YOU want to work for.

Guidelines for planning and surviving a second and subsequent interviews

Here are some important guidelines to consider when planning for a second or subsequent interview. The stakes are higher so there's more pressure on both you and the organization. No one wants to make a mistake.

Scheduling your appointment

When scheduling the interview, always clarify the schedule and agenda. These interviews typically are longer and involve discussions with several people in the organization. Always find out who will interview you. Will you have sequential interviews with key decision-makers or will you meet with a group?

Preparing for individual interviews

Preparing for sequential interviews is much like the process you used to prepare for your initial interview with one major difference. At this stage of the process, interviewers will assess you on your ability to do the job as well as how well you FIT with the organization. They are looking for traits and personality cues that will help them decide if they can work with you – if the chemistry is right. A final hiring decision is made based on how well they perceive you'll fit in the organization. It's not based on skills and abilities.

It's important to know exactly who you'll be meeting with, their position in the organization, why they are part of the interview process, and the time allocated for each. Have two or three customized questions for each person.

Use the same listening and attending techniques discussed earlier in this chapter.

NOTES

Guidelines

- Schedule your appointment.

- Prepare for individual interview.

- Prepare for group interview

- Prepare your questions.

Preparing for group interviews

Group or panel interviews serve two purposes. First, it speeds up the interview process. Second, it allows the group to hear your responses and discuss them as a group after you've left. A group interview may feel that it's "you against them." In many ways this is unavoidable because there is only one of you and several of "them."

Here's some suggestions that will help you manage the group interview and turn it into a valuable job-search tool:

1. Prior to the interview, ask your contact for the names and titles of those who will participate. Also, ask how the group plans to make their final hiring decision. Will there be one person who will decide with input from the group or is it a group decision? You must know their decision-making process BEFORE the interview. Plan your questions and approach accordingly.

2. Try to get a reading on who carries the "power" in the group. This is tough to assess before an interview. Be aware that a certain person in the group may not be responsible for the final hiring decision, but has clout with the group. Watch for any "power plays" before the interview and early on.

3. Never agree to a group interview that's scheduled over lunch or dinner. There are too many distractions. It's okay to have lunch or dinner as a wrap-up to an interview. (See point 4 below for my thoughts on how to handle food during an interview.)

4. Introduce yourself to everyone before the interview begins. Shake hands and ask what department they are with. There will usually be some kind of food, coffee and soft drinks available. My suggestion – politely reject offers of food, coffee or soft drinks; always choose water. You are there to work, not eat

and drink. Coffee may dry out your mouth and you don't want to be chewing while answering a question. You can always have something after the interview. Have water available to keep your mouth moist. Use a hard candy just before the interview to moisten your throat.

5. Ask each person to introduce themselves including name, how long they've been with the organization, their title, and what they "really" do. Either make a mental note of each person or, what is more helpful, quickly draw a seating chart with first names. This helps you to respond on a first–name basis later in the interview and to address certain questions to the most appropriate individuals.

6. Someone will moderate the interview and probably ask the first question. Expect this person to clarify information throughout the interview.

7. Each group member will probably ask pre–assigned questions. These questions will usually apply to their area of expertise or responsibility within the organization. This is why it's helpful to have a diagram – a quick glance at it and you can frame your response or subsequent question accordingly.

    When someone asks a question, look directly at them, then gradually look around the table at the other members. This technique acknowledges everyone's interest in each response and helps develop a feeling of team spirit while, at the same time, acknowledging and responding to the person who asked the question. This gives you the opportunity to "talk to" each individual in the group.

8. Look for ways to connect a response to something someone said earlier in the interview. This shows your ability to integrate thoughts and ideas – a strength.

9. Conclude the interview by asking the moderator to describe the process they'll use to evaluate candidates. State that you'll follow-up in a few days. Be sure you know who to contact.

10. Send a follow-up thank-you letter to the moderator. Indicate the next action steps you'll take. Review any points that came up during the interview that are a good match to your skills and abilities. Acknowledge those in the group who you felt you "connected" with.

Preparing questions to ask during the later interviews

As you prepare questions for these interviews, remember that you are making a decision on what should be a long-term relationship. You and your employer will form a relationship where each provides a valuable contribution to each others welfare. To help in your decision process, plan for and ask carefully considered questions. Spend time preparing challenging questions for your interviewers so you will better understand the position, the organization, its people and culture.

Here's examples of questions to use in group or individual interviews. They can be directed at each person's area of expertise. You can compare responses to look for consistencies in values, mission, vision and future direction. These questions can also be used if you are interviewing with a newly formed organization:

Strategy questions

1. What are the goals for this organization? ;
2. What were the goals for creating this organization?;
3. What are the priorities for the first year?;
4. How will you measure success after the first year? After the third year?;
5. How will you measure success of the person in this position after the first year? Third year?;

262

6. What do you feel are the biggest hurdles for the organization in the first year? In the third year? Why?; and

7. Is the goal of this organization to break-even or to make a profit?

Service questions

8. Describe the services that this organization is providing?;
9. Describe the businesses the various entities might be involved in? (e.g., eye care, free-standing surgery centers, any sub–specialty); and
10. Describe the types of positions that you anticipate you'll be hiring in the future? Why?

Financial questions

11. What is the source of capital to operate the organization?;
12. What are the projections of capital needs for the first two – three years?;
13. Where will additional capital come from if the availability does not meet projections?; and
14. Do you have a pro forma?

Governance questions

15. Describe the ownership;
16. Describe how the buy-in to the organization happens;
17. Describe the roles of the board, any commit-tees and the executive director; and
18. Does this position have a vote and stock on the board?

General questions

19. What is your management style?;
20. If we disagree, how would we settle it?;
21. What happened to the last person who had this job?;

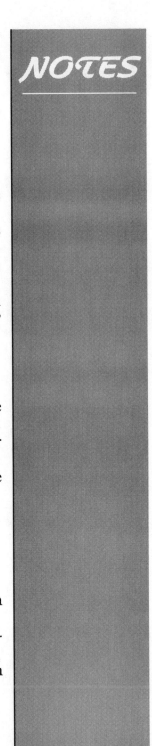

22. What have been the primary reasons for people leaving this job?;
23. How do you evaluate performance?;
24. What sort of people do you have difficulty working with?;
25. How are promotions determined?;
26. How are decisions made?;
27. How receptive is this organization to new ideas?;
28. How do you like people to communicate with you?;
29. Who are the other people I'd be working with? When might I talk with them?;
30. Describe the benefit package;
31. Is there a bonus plan? What would it take to explore starting a bonus plan?;
32. What kind of severance plan do you have?;
33. Do you have a home purchase plan? Describe it; and
34. Do you cover relocation costs? Describe the plan.

Use the space below to add any of your own favorite questions.

-
-
-
-
-

Final thoughts about interviews

After all interviews are compete, interviewers will meet to discuss reactions and observations. Remember one critical point: their analysis and subsequent selection **won't be based on reasons to hire you**. Instead, the discussion will focus on **reasons to eliminate you.** You probably haven't thought about it from this perspective. Think back to some of the hiring decisions you've been involved in. What was the discussion? It focused on how people didn't have certain qualifications or personality traits, etc. A final decision is reached by the group eliminating candidates. Also, the final decision is typically not based on a candidate's skill and qualifications – it's usually emotional. Interviewers ask themselves two questions: 1) Can I (we) work with this person; and 2) Will they fit in to our culture, our organization?

As you prepare for an interview, ask yourself these same questions: 1) Do I feel I can work with these people?; and 2) Is their culture one that matches my values and personality?

Don't forget. **YOU** are in charge of your job search. **YOU** have the power to accept or decline an offer. It's **YOUR** decision.

Chapter 7

Take charge of your negotiation

Don't worry, you're really an expert at negotiation. You've been doing it all your life. In fact, you started negotiating before you learned to walk. As a child, you negotiated when you wanted food, even before you could talk; you negotiated with your parents how long you could stay outside and play with friends after dark or when you could go to bed on special nights. As a teenager, you negotiated when you could take driving lessons, in some cases being so successful that you talked at least one parent into letting you practice before you had your temporary permit. Then came the difficult negotiation – getting the family car for Saturday night once you had your license. Finally, as an adult, you negotiate with family, employers, employees and colleagues every day of the year, over a variety of large and small issues.

See, you really are an expert in negotiation. Why then do we usually fear this part of the job search? Because it's a skill we don't use every day – we think we're not very good at it. And, besides, it seems more difficult because stakes are higher; you're negotiating your compensation package and job responsibilities..

The following ideas and techniques are meant to provide that little boost of confidence to competently negotiate a job offer that meets your personal and professional needs as well as those of the hiring organization.

Negotiation is an art, but it's an art you can learn and do better if you understand:

• What negotiation really is;
• The critical steps to negotiating job offers; and
• When, what and how to negotiate.

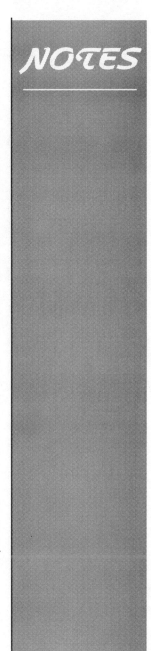

Negotiation

- Identify expectations.

- Define roles, responsibilities.

- Build trust, strength.

What is negotiation?

The phone rings, the person you've been interviewing with is on the line, your heart races, and YES, she offers you the position. Your immediate reaction – accept the offer! After all, that's been your goal. And you don't know if you'll get another offer soon.

But wait – don't rush into acceptance. First, decide if the offer is right for you – if the position and organization will provide the environment and work that will meet or exceed your needs and match your career goal.

According to *Webster's New College Dictionary*, negotiation is *to confer with another so as to arrive at the settlement of some matter. It's the action or process of negotiating or being negotiated.* Thus, in negotiating a job offer, you and the employer must reach a mutual agreement, through discussion, on all terms of employment. And you must do so without damaging the relationship you've developed up to this point.

Negotiating the final offer is more than just getting the salary and benefits you want. That means you must:

1. Identify and clarify expectations with your future boss – the organization's *and* yours. Don't wait until AFTER you've accepted and started the job. You may uncover an expectation that you haven't discussed but is serious enough to affect your decision.

    Here's one example: After being on the job for only two weeks, a practice manager found that the organization expected him to be on call at least two weekends each month. They had discussed the possibility of "on-call" status during interviews, but had never clearly defined what it meant. He assumed it meant responding to an occasional page if a problem came up. Surprisingly, the organization defined "on-call" as being on the site two

Saturdays a month and in town on Sunday of that same weekend so he could respond to emergencies. This meant he had to stay close to the phone – not just at the other end of a pager. After three months he resigned.

2. Clearly define the roles and responsibilities as they relate to the organization's overall goals and objectives. It's critical for you, as a new practice manager, to clearly understand and agree with short- and long-term goals.

3. Enter discussions from a foundation of trust and strength. Trust is the result of all your work building a relationship with the employer up to this point. Strength means how well your experience and skills match the organization's needs and requirements. Trust and strength build from the ideas discussed throughout this book.

Evaluate the offer

Consider four critical areas:

1) Roles, responsibilities, expectations;

2) Resources available to you;

3) Rewards and outcomes or results; and

4) Obstacles – obvious and hidden.

Ask yourself the following questions for each of the four areas. Do you have enough information or clear answers to each? Should you be asking yourself other questions and subsequently, asking the employer?

Roles, responsibilities, expectations

• What are the hiring manager's expectations? The organization's? Are the deadlines realistic?

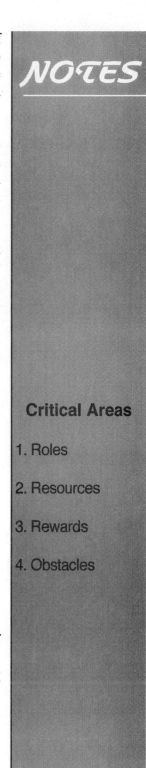

NOTES

Critical Areas

1. Roles

2. Resources

3. Rewards

4. Obstacles

269

- To whom will you report? If it is a Board, will one person be your direct boss? Is there a committee? If there is a committee, what are its dynamics?

- Who will evaluate your performance? Do you know the criteria? What are the measurement criteria? What is your role in the performance review?

- What really is the scope of your authority? Does it match your responsibility?

Resources available to you

- Are the resources enough to meet the expectations, roles and responsibilities?

- Is there a detailed budget? Is it approved? If not, why? What is the organization's budget history? Is it reluctant to spend money to upgrade facilities and equipment? Why?

- Does the administrative staff have the tools and resources to do their job? Are the tools or resources out of date? Is there a budget to upgrade them?

Rewards, outcomes, results

- How does the organization recognize and reward outstanding performance?

- What will the organization do to help you with your professional development? Continuing education? Certification?

- What is the policy for reimbursing expenses?

- Do you understand the entire benefit package?

- Have any physicians left the practice? What was the reason? and

- How many new physicians are on staff? What is the plan for hiring?

Obstacles – obvious and hidden

- What is the organization's financial position? What are their plans and goals for the next two or three years?

- What is the current situation of the senior board members? Are any nearing retirement? If so, how might that affect the group and your position?

- Why is this position open? Was there a person previously in the position? Why did they leave? If it's a new position, why was it created? and

- Where is the previous person now? Should you talk to him or her?

What other questions can you think of? Use the space below to list them.

-

-

-

-

-

Follow clear steps in your negotiation

As you negotiate, keep in mind these key points:

1. View negotiation as win - win.

Always view a negotiation as a win-win situation; you both want to reach the same goal. Recognize this is the beginning of a long, positive relationship that must meet both parties' needs. Be sure you know the employer's needs; never become

adversarial. If a negotiation becomes adversarial, there may be larger issues. Step back and look again at the entire situation. It may not be right for you or the organization.

2. Be clear about your needs.

Know exactly what your needs are. Having a career plan, including a personal mission or purpose statement, helps you evaluate the final offer in specific terms. You must be very clear on your expectations concerning job specifications, role and responsibility for outcomes. You must clearly understand your personal values – what you'll compromise if need be and what you won't. You must clearly understand interests and skills that truly energize and motivate you. Ask yourself, "Is this a job that will motivate me to jump out of bed before the alarm on a Monday morning?

3.   Remember, everything is negotiable.

Negotiation can, and should, include more than just salary and benefits. Following is a list of things you could negotiate:

> Bonus
> Profit sharing
> Expense account
> Medical and dental insurance
> Vacation
> Tax/legal consulting
> Country club memberships
> Athletic club memberships
> Deferred compensation
> Various sick leave options
> Travel
> Equity options
> Company car
> Life insurance
> Retirement funds
> Annual physical exams
> Professional development opportunities
> Severance and outplacement services
> Relocation expenses
> Parental leave

Can you think of any other items?

4. *Know that you don't have to accept (or decline) the offer during negotiations*

In fact, don't accept (or decline) an offer during negotiations. Take time to think about the final offer (what you've negotiated). You will need this time to reflect on how well the offer will match your career goal(s) and expectations. You also need time to discuss it with your family. Get the final offer in writing. You don't want any misunderstanding once you accept it.

5. *Consider your needs for relocating.*

If the offer requires relocation out of state, you must negotiate at least one visit, and preferably two, with your family for house hunting and getting the general lay of the land. If you're married or have children, your family must be intimately involved in the final decision, giving their opinions on housing, schools, environment, etc. If you have a working spouse, you need to research employment opportunities for him or her.

6. *Negotiate flexibly.*

Don't set yourself up for failure with a lot of un-negotiable requirements. I know someone who actually turned down an offer because the organization wouldn't agree to five weeks of vacation during the first year of employment. If you are stuck on one point, I suggest leaving that point and going on to another. You may need to concede one point in order to gain something more critical in the long run.

If you continue "stuck" on a point, you may need to clarify with yourself just how important it is to you in the long term. I've seen clients get stuck on a difference of $2000 in yearly salary. If they step back and see that translates to only $167 per month less taxes, it may not be a major issue.

273

7. Clearly articulate your needs and requirements.

Clearly communicate your needs, requirements, and expectations. Don't assume. If some detail is unclear, ask for clarification. Be straightforward and specific about your concerns – what you are looking for and what you want out of the relationship. It helps to write out your expectations before you get to the negotiation table. Take notes into the meeting, so you don't forget anything.

8. Negotiate benefits and incentives.

Negotiate benefits only after you agree to a base salary. Salary and benefits are two different issues, so treat them as such. Never accept what appears to be a standard benefit package; you can usually enhance your individual package to meet any unique needs and requirements. I've had clients negotiate medical benefit packages because a family member had a special medical problem that required special treatment or longer care. As a rule, smaller organizations tend to have more flexible benefit packages, but they may not be able to afford more benefits.

9. Negotiate salary.

Yep, this is the difficult negotiation step. Negotiating salary usually scares most people. However, it's been my experience that, if you follow the process described in this book, it naturally flows into salary, and the discussion is easy. Here are some ideas to keep in mind as you "negotiate" salary.

Once the organization has given a salary figure or a range, it can negotiate upward. Once you give a salary range, you can negotiate only downward. Remember, the manager's job is to try to hire you at the lowest reasonable salary; it's your job to try to get yourself hired at the highest reasonable salary. That's why a general rule-of-thumb is to hold off talking about salary for as long as you can. The ideal situation is to have the offer on the table before talking salary. If the salary comes up before you know enough about the position, ask to hold off until you understand it better and the organization knows better how your qualifications match their requirements.

Throughout the interview process, you want to learn how much flexibility and power the person you're negotiating with has. You must negotiate the complete compensation package with the decision-maker – the person who can make the final decision. I've often seen candidates negotiate with the person who would be their boss, thinking they could get a final decision, only to find out the package just agreed to has to be approved by someone else – perhaps even the entire board or an executive committee. Many negotiations fall apart at this point.

If you are not sure of the decision-making power of the person you're talking with, be direct: ask if he or she can make the final decision or if others must approve what you negotiate. If others must approve, ask to discuss salary directly with that authority.

Also, if a position carries an advertised salary range, recognize that organizations typically have a 10-20 percent flex above that range. Don't assume you have to accept the published salary figure. In fact, that's the value of interviewing and matching your skills to their requirements. The more you demonstrate your value, the greater the chances are that they will increase their initial offer.

Should the organization's final salary offer still be lower than what you were anticipating, here's one suggestion that might help. Most organizations have some kind of probation period (usually six months) after which they usually make a salary adjustment. I've suggested and have had many clients successfully negotiate a probation period of two or three months. These clients established objectives related to the organization's short-term needs, that if met, would lead to a salary adjustment. In most cases, this type of arrangement met both the needs of my clients and the organization.

275

In addition, I've had clients successfully negotiate quarterly performance review updates with related salary adjustments – in place of the dreaded annual review, which most bosses forget or ignore anyway. I've found salary adjustments are easier if you can continually up-date your boss on your progress and accomplishments, as they happen, and relate them directly to bottom line.

There are probably hundreds of other creative ways to solve the centuries-old salary dilemma. You've just got to get creative. What other creative ideas do you have? I'd love to hear about them.

10. Finally, decide.

Here are the major things to consider when making the final decision:

- Carefully review all self-discovery work you've done, including your personal mission statement. How closely does the final offer match to your mission? Is it a match? If so, GREAT! If not, where does is differ? Is the difference significant enough for you to reconsider? Analyze!;

- How closely does this offer match your career goal(s)?;

- Does the offer give you the chance to use skills that truly energize and motivate you?

- Can you honestly say that by taking this job you would be so excited to work that on Monday mornings you'd "fly" out of bed before the alarm just because you were excited about getting to work. Or would you find it difficult to quit work Friday evenings because you were so "involved" in what you were doing. If you feel as though it would be a struggle just to come to work, then this may not be the opportunity for you;

- How well will the job fit with your family's life style?; and

- Are the negatives significant or insignificant compared to all the positives? Analyze!

The best advice I can give when it comes to making a decision, listen to your gut instincts; they don't lie.

Get the offer in writing

You've just concluded a successful negotiation: you and the organization have reached an oral agreement and heads have nodded on everything discussed. Do you accept the offer? Consider that you've just finished negotiating for the position, the compensation package (including salary, bonus or incentive, benefits and perquisites), a schedule for performance reviews and a start date. That's quite a bit of information to assimilate and accurately remember. No, you don't decide yet! Instead, ask for the terms in writing. Any number of things can happen between the negotiation discussion and what appears on paper.

Be sure the confirmation letter includes job title, start date and all other terms of employment as negotiated and agreed to. If you don't get a letter, write your own letter detailing all arrangements and agreements and send it to your contact.

Once you have the final offer on paper and in hand, you can review the complete package and decide. It's customary to ask for two to five days to review the written offer.

Once you have decided to accept the offer, contact the person hiring you. It's okay to accept the offer over the phone and mail a signed copy. If it's a local job, I recommend hand-carrying the signed copy to the person hiring you. Keep a signed and dated copy for yourself.

Keep your job search moving

Do not stop your job search until you have a signed contract and have agreed to a start date. In one recent example, a client had oral commitments from two different academic group practices, both out of state. In the course of two days this client saw both offers vaporize.

In one case, the final offer was all but made. The hiring administrator wanted my client to have one last group interview with the department heads he would be working with. This would be the fourth interview, on-site and my client was to bring his spouse along so they could house hunt. In fact, a realtor met them at the airport. However, during the group interview, one person voiced concern that since he was not involved in the earlier interviews, he wouldn't approve the offer to my client. Without a unanimous vote by the group, the hiring manager backed down and withdrew the offer. The devastating thing is that this negative individual would not have direct contact with my client. He just felt "miffed" not to be included in the initial screening. The lucky part of the story is that my client and his wife hadn't sign a contract on a house – they took a contract home with them to review but wanted to wait until they had a contract in hand before committing to a house.

Within 24 hours, the second academic practice called and withdrew its offer because it suddenly felt obligated to offer the position to an inside person. Oh yes, the organization knew about this person all along; the interviewers simply didn't tell my client, always indicating he was the front-runner for the position.

Devastating as these two events were, my client had kept his search active, so he was able to continue as though these two situations had not happened. Emotionally, it was a draining experience, but he had to regroup. As of this writing, this same client is awaiting confirmation from another offer. By the way, it will turn out to be a much better situation, professionally and financially, for him and his family.

Had this client stopped his job search when an offer seemed assured, he would have needed two to three weeks to jump-start his search. As it was, he was able to hit the ground running, once he got over the shock and devastation.

The morale of this story: Keep your job search active and healthy. Don't prematurely announce the offer beyond your family and friends. More important, don't give in to the temptation to put everything else on hold until you have a final, signed contract.

What about employment contracts?

A common question I continually hear in today's market is "Should I request some sort of employment contract?" Generally, medical group boards and chief executive officers don't like employment contracts. Philosophically, I don't like them either. However, suppose you sense that the job opportunity entails some risk for you, such as relocation or an environment that is in a state of chaos due to mergers and integrations. In this case, you must be able to financially protect yourself and your family. You can't be expected to move across the country to a new job in a chaotic environment without some financial security.

Here's a true story that illustrates this point. I had just started some consulting work to help a major medical center in the western United States lessen the effects of downsizing on its staff. The new director of nursing services had started her new job that same day, after having relocated from the East Coast. And on the very same day – her first day on the job – she was told her job had been eliminated. If she chose, she would interview for any other position within the

NOTES

medical center. Or she was free to leave. Here was a single parent with two kids who had just relocated two-thirds of the way across the country, signed a lease on a house, and suddenly was without a job. Situations like this one make me say that managers and administrators must have employment agreements – without exception.

The following information outlines some of my thoughts and experience in using employment contracts. If you should decide to negotiate a contract, I strongly suggest you find a local attorney who specializes in them. Here's one caution – before mentioning a contract to a board or CEO, be sure you're very clear on why you need one, how it would benefit the employer, and the specific needs you want included in it.

Several clients have been more successful by not referring to an employment contract by that name. They used terms like *employment agreement, statement of understanding* or *agreement*. One client even used the phrase, "how we will work together." Because "contract" seems to be a "dirty word" to most CEOs and boards, you may have to come up with your own creative name for it.

Why managers and administrators need employment contracts

The environment that managers and administrators work in today means we must redefine the roles and responsibilities in health care organizations. Administrators will succeed or fail by their ability to provide comprehensive, synergistic leadership; innovative management strategies; and significant investments in time.

In this environment an employment contract can motivate positive changes. This legal document forms the organization's parameters for an administrator's authority, responsibility and accountability; it also commits the organizational support necessary to succeed. If one of these factors is limited or not clearly defined in formal employment contracts or informal agreements, success is possible but more difficult to achieve.[1]

I wish a hand shake and good faith could complete all agreements. But I also recognize the world of health care is much too volatile for this old approach. Thus, I'm finding more and more managers use employment contracts once an offer is on the table and negotiations are down to crossing the "Ts" and dotting the "Is."

What typical employment contracts leave out

Reviewing examples of actual administrator employment contracts reveals some typical sections. These come from organizations of all sizes and include group practices with single and multiple specialties:

    Manager performance evaluation
    Agreement not assignable
    Arbitration
    Authorities
    Automobile liability insurance
    Benefits and reimbursements
    Compensation
    Confidentiality
    Disability insurance
    Duties (roles and responsibilities)
    Employer-employee relationship
    Fidelity bond
    Indemnification
    Leave time
    Organizational policies and procedures
    Retirement
    Standard contract terms - examples
    Terms of employment
    Termination
    Yearly manager physical evaluations

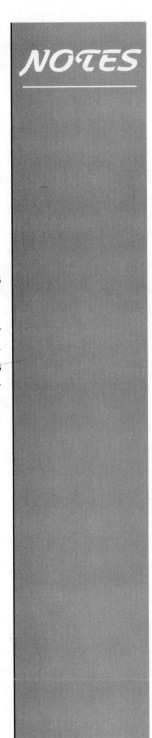

---

[1] Administrator Employment Contract; Volume III in the MGMA Series of Strategic Agreements; C. Kay Freeman; MGMA; 1989.

But current economic conditions require managers to add two important sections:

1) Severance policy in case employment ends; and

2) Provisions for outplacement services.

I rarely see these two provisions in contracts, but you must include them to protect yourself financially. Even the board won't be aware of everything that may (will) affect managers in the future.

These provisions are especially critical if you relocate to another state or region of the country. Your employment status may unexpectedly change. Your group could become involved in an integration or merger, which would create redundant managers or administrators. Physicians could decide to sell to another physician group. Any number of changes could affect you. Your job is to show the CEO and board how important these two sections are.

Contracts should include severance pay

Some readers will think my recommendations are excessive, but I don't believe they are when you consider the fact that the average job search takes about nine months. It can take longer if you are relocating and have to begin a job search in an area where you don't have a network established.

For those who have relocated to a different part of the country (and are conducting a job search), I recommend the following sliding scale which protects you if your new job suddenly changes or is eliminated.

Job lost during first year of employment:

I recommend one year in severance pay with full medical benefits. Medical benefits may be negotiated such as full medical benefits for the manager and COBRA benefits for family members, or six months of full family coverage, not the full 12 months of coverage.

Job lost during second year of employment:

I recommend six months of severance pay and six to 12 months of medical insurance. Again medical benefits might be negotiated.

I suggest shifting strategy after the third year of employment. At this point there shouldn't be any "unexpected" decisions that impact you. Instead, I think you need to start accumulating severance time because of length of service to your group or organization.

Job lost after three to six years of service:

I recommend at least six months of severance pay and six months of continued family medical benefits. I've seen some agreements where the severance is nine months to one year at full salary with benefits.

Job lost after six years to eight years of service:

I recommend 12 months of severance pay and 12 months of family medical benefits. In some cases, I've seen nine months although I feel this is too modest.

Job lost after more than eight years of service:

I recommend at least 12 months severance and 12 months of medical benefits.

NOTES

Contracts should include funds for outplacement

You should also write into the employment agreement funds for working with an outplacement consultant. No matter how well connected you may be, it's always a benefit to work with someone who can help you jump-start your job search. A consultant can help you organize your job-search plan and continually motivate you throughout your search. It's helpful to have another person review your resume and cover letters as well as help you practice and hone your interviewing skills.

Usually $2500 to $4000 is enough to cover outplacement consulting. In some cases, clients haven't specified a dollar amount in the employment contract. Instead, they include a statement indicating that they will interview two or three outplacement companies and select one. In this case, the agreement may contain a "not-to-exceed" dollar figure. If you use a not-to-exceed figure, I suggest $5000. That should cover most outplacement consulting fees.

For executive positions, depending on the size of the group or hospital, I've seen outplacement budgets from $15,000 to $20,000 per person. The higher figures usually are for executives who have been with an organization for more than ten years and may be responsible for large financial budgets.

Contracts may be negotiable later

Remember, everything is negotiable, so get creative when you've lost your job. One client, who lost his job because of a merger had initially received six months severance. Five months of organized job search had resulted in six or seven leads but no job offers. I suggested he go back to his former group, describe the job-search work he had done over the five months, and request three more months severance. He thought I was nuts but then decided he didn't have anything to lose.

284

Result: He got two more months severance. By the way, I've also several clients who've had identical requests turned down. But in two of these cases, the CEO suggested other colleagues my client could network with. In these instances, both clients connected with people who had contacts that eventually led to job offers. The moral of this story: Never say never – it never hurts to ask, and you never know what other useful information you may uncover.

You've signed the contract and set a start date but you're still not done

There are still a few loose ends to tie up. First and foremost, be sure to contact all the people who made you offers or with whom you have had extensive negotiations Thank them and inform them of your decision. Make it clear that you are not rejecting them, but have simply selected the job that better matched your career goals and personal mission.

Second, be sure to tell all the network contacts who have been so important and helpful in your job search. Notify all your references. For those who have had significant input or have been a major help in your search, a personal phone call is appropriate. Be sure to follow up your phone call with a written note including your new title, business address, and phone number. For those who have been helpful but not critical to your search, a personal thank-you note informing them about your new job offer is very appropriate; include your new title, business address and phone number.

In each and every case make it clear that you intend to keep them updated on your progress and look forward to a continuing professional relationship. It's critical that you continue to maintain your professional network – you never know what your future has in store for you.

And finally, you can celebrate. Congratulations!

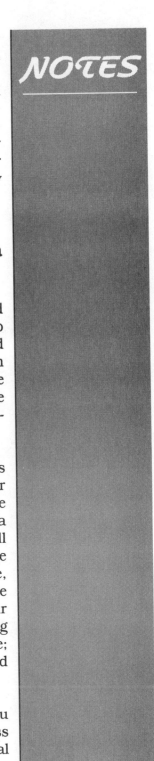

Some recommended references and resources

There are literally thousands of career and job-search related publications on the market today. I've listed just a few of the ones that I feel provide information in a way that relates to the ideas and techniques I've addressed in the book.

The following list should help take some of the confusion out of your job search. Some of the publications can be found in the business or reference section of your public library.

Read about trends in the industry of your choice

1. *Occupational Outlook Handbook;* Compiled by the United States Department of Labor; 1996-1997 Edition VGM Career Horizons; NTC Publishing Group.

    Publication that describes what workers do on the job, the working conditions, the training and education needed, earnings and expected job prospects in approximately 250 occupations.

2. *Dictionary of Occupational Titles;* Combined Volume I & II; Fourth Edition, Revised 1991; JIST Works, Inc., Indianapolis, IN.

    This book is a complete reprint of the Dictionary of Occupational Titles as produced by the US Department of Labor. It includes all the content of the original. This

NOTES

edition describes more than 12,000 occupations, detailing typical tasks and listing education needed.

Guide to executive recruiters

3. *The Directory of Executive Recruiters 1998;* 27th Edition; Kennedy Information, LLC.

    A comprehensive reference on executive recruiters throughout the country. Includes more than 3700 search firms, cross-indexed by management function, geography and industry.

Myers-Briggs applied to career planning

4. *Do What You Are: Discover the Perfect Career for You Through the Secrets of Personality Type;* Second Edition; Paul D. Tieger & Barbara Barron-Tieger; Little, Brown and Company; 1995.

5. *Manual: A Guide to the Development and Use of the Myers-Briggs Type Indicator;* Isabel Briggs Myers and Mary H. McCaulley; Consulting Psychologists Press, Inc.; 1985.

Career planning and development; change and transitions

6. *Zen and the Art of Making A Living: A practical guide to creative career design;* Laurence G. Boldt; The Penguin Group, Penguin Books USA, Inc.; 1993.

7. *How to find the work you love;* Laurence G. Boldt; The Penguin Group, Penguin Books USA, Inc.; 1996.

8. *Job Shift: How to prosper in a workplace without jobs;* William Bridges; Addison-Wesley Publishing Company; 1994.

9. *Managing Transitions: Making the most of change;* William Bridges; Addison-Wesley Publishing Company; 1991.

10. *Transitions: Making sense of life's changes;* William Bridges; Addison-Wesley Publishing Company; 1980.

11. *Work in the NEW Economy; Career and job seeking into the 21st century;* Revised Edition; Robert Wegmann, Robert Chapman, and Miriam Johnson; American Association for Counseling and Development & JIST Works, Inc.; 1989.

Electronic job search

12. *Career Xroads: The 1997 Directory to Job, Resume, and Career Management Sites on the World Wide Web;* Gerry Crispin and Mark Mehler; MMC Group; 1997.

13. *Using the Internet and the World Wide Web in your Job Search: The complete guide to on-line job seeking and career information;* Fred E. Jandy & Mary B. Nemnich; JIST Works, Inc.; 1997.

Internet web sites

There are dozens of career-related web sites on the Web. New ones are added daily; some disappear. The few I've listed below were valid sites as of May 1998. Continue to browse the Web for new and improved sites. Your best strategy is to test each major site and stick with those that return the most pertinent job leads. Explore the following sites:

NOTES

14. *CareerPath* (http://www.careerpath.com). This site contains classified job listings from dozens of US daily newspapers and has an easily executed search engine. It may be the best overall site for general job hunting. Approximately 250,000 jobs are listed. You can focus your search by region or industry.

15. *Career Mosaic* (http://www.careermosaic. com). This site typically has over 70,000 jobs listed. Its services are free to job seekers. You can scan the listings and even post your resume for potential employers to see. It provides industry-specific listings.

16. *Hover's OnLine* (http://www.hovers.com). This site offers profiles and financial data on more than 12,000 public and private companies worldwide. It provides links to other free sites when you can explore even more.

17. *NationJob Network* (http:///www.nationjob. com). You can enter your personal profile of your ideal job – location, salary and industry. Provide your e-mail address and wait for appropriate listings to be sent to you.

20. *Resume Bank* (http://www.resumail.com). This is a resource employers use when searching for qualified applicants.

21. *Yahoo search engine* (http://www.yahoo.com/ Business/Employment/). This is Yahoo's gateway to employment-related web sites.

In addition, most companies and organizations with web sites post job listings. Many have jobs or career opportunities as a menu option. Most company web sites include relevant information about the company. Some provide links to other useful information.

This list is small. There are hundreds of others. Start searching. I'd like to hear if you find others you feel are worthwhile and useful.

Review of the important ideas and techniques

Chapter 1: Why I should read this book

1. My theme is simple – take control of your career. This means being "career resilient." Gone are the days when you could trade your loyalty to an employer and hard work for job security and steady promotions. You can't depend on (or expect) your organization, large or small, to manage your career for you. Instead, you must manage your own career – a responsibility that requires much of you.

2. Your journey for taking control of your career and the decisions that affect your career begins with you. Identifying your personal mission and then diligently planning to move toward it is the first, yet critical, step in taking control of your career.

3. You've learned specific strategies and techniques to:

    •   Prepare yourself to take control of your job search;

    •   Identify key parts of a self-marketing portfolio;

    •   Develop your resume database, which you'll use to customize cover letters and resumes, prepare marketing letters, and plan for and conduct interviews confidently and competently;

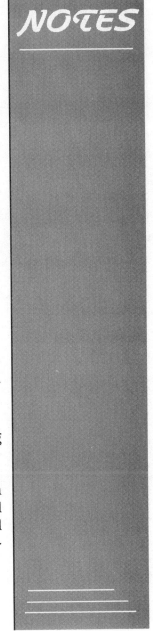

- Continually research ways to meet the needs (requirements) of the hiring organization – at every step in the job search;

- Demonstrate how your experiences, background and accomplishments MATCH an organization's needs, qualifications and requirements;

- Put your needs and requirements "on the back burner" during the search, at least until the second and third interview;

- Confidently negotiate a final offer that successfully meets your requirements, as well as the hiring organization's needs; and

- Suggest and write employment contracts that protect you and the hiring organization.

Chapter 2: Take charge of your career

1. Obstacles to managing my career:

   - Procrastination;

   - Fear of change;

   - Reluctance to give up what you have and know;

   - Lack of knowledge about yourself; and

   - Lack of personal career planning and goal setting.

2. Techniques you can use to take charge:

   - Continually update your education and training;

   - Think "project," not job;

   - Add value to the organization;

- Develop a short-term plan for contingencies; and

- Develop a long-term career plan and objectives:

  * Discover your career self;
  * Define your career goal(s); and
  * Develop your career plan(s).

Chapter 3: Take charge of marketing yourself

1. Understanding yourself:

   - Develop clear career goals and plans by answering three questions:

     * Who am I?;
     * Where am I going?; and
     * How do I get to where I want to go?

   - Know what you are selling. As you prepare to market yourself, it's critical to understand exactly what it is you are selling. In a single word – you are selling "YOU!" It's useful to think in terms of five Vs when marketing yourself: value, volition, versatility, visibility and vision.

2. Develop your resume database:

   - A resume database is one document that contains accomplishments and achievements from your entire work history. List every company you've worked with, all volunteer activities, and any personal activities. Your objective in developing a resume database is to write a short, yet descriptive story for each accomplishment, task or project. Each story should be two - three sentences describing what you did and any outcome or result for each activity. Don't worry about length or wordiness. Brainstorm every aspect of

NOTES

each assignment, project, task, etc. Don't be concerned with the length. A typical database could be 10 to 25 pages.

- Use your database to customize resumes, cover letters, marketing letters, and to prepare for interviews.

- Use two key questions to shape your database stories:

  * What did I do when I did that?; and,
  * So what?

3. Consider six alternatives for your job search:

- Networking: Identifying and using your personal contacts;
- Directing marketing letters to selected companies or individual;
- Working with executive search firms;
- Responding to ads in newspapers and professional trade journals;
- Making "cold" calls; and
- Old fashioned luck.

Chapter 4: Take charge of your selling tools I: Sharpen your resume

1. Your resume is really a proposal. Consider your resume a proposal document in which you're proposing yourself as a solution to a prospective employer's problem and need.

2. There's a catch. Your resume must grab the attention of the reader, to persuade the reader to pick up the phone and call – **in 15 seconds.** Yes, that's right, 15 seconds. Your resume has 15 seconds to persuade the reader to action.

3. Your strategy? Use your resume database to customize every cover letter and resume:

- Include accomplishment statements from your database that are a close match with the reader needs;

- Prioritize your accomplishment statements – list them in a way that sets them apart from your other statements; and

- Include more detailed information with those accomplishments that match the requirements. You may end up with accomplishment statements that are in outline form – one main point followed by four or five detailed sub-points.

4. Tips and tactics for fine-tuning your resume:

- Length: Do not limit yourself to a one-, two- or three-page resume. Including cover letter, your resume can be longer. As you know, it's physically impossible to summarize five, ten, even 15 years of experience on one or two pages. So don't! Besides, the reader will make the first screen-in decision in that 15 seconds;

- Layout: Should provide for quick and easy scanning. Organize your information in such a way that helps the reader *find* your key quickly and easily;

- Active writing style: Language used in your resume must be crisp, succinct, yet personal. The words you use must illustrate both results through activity and energy;

- Avoid using "I": Avoid repeated use of "I" at the beginning of sentences and accomplishment statements;

- Proofread. There is only one rule when it comes to typos: NO typos or errors of any kind – period! Meticulously read and re-read your written work. Ask someone unfamiliar with the material to proofread;

- Use quality paper. Many so-called experts suggest using different colored paper or a different/unique type style to make your resume and cover letter stand out. I don't! Use a high quality, white paper stock;

- Choosing a font. Select a font that is professional and easy to read. New Times Roman or Arial are excellent types if you use a PC. Macintosh users will find Palatino an excellent choice. Consider Arial Bold for subheadings; and

- Faxing resumes. Most organizations and groups accept faxed resumes. In fact, most classified ads include a fax number. Whenever you fax a cover letter/resume, ALWAYS mail a clean copy of the exact same material.

5. What not to include in your resume. This is simple – don't include any information that could *potentially* screen you out. Here are the general categories of information to omit:

    - Salary history/requirements;

    - Reasons for leaving your previous job;

    - Availability date;

    - Location preference;

    - Resume preparation date; and

    - Personal information about your family or your photo.

6. Resume formats. There are three generally accepted formats: 1) chronological; 2) functional; and 3) the marketing letter. You've heard experts recommend the chronological format and discourage the functional format. I don't agree with this argument. I suggest selecting the format that BEST fits each dif-

ferent situation. Remember, your objective is to demonstrate how your experience matches the needs of that particular opportunity. In one case, you may decide the chronological format is best. In another case, a marketing letter is appropriate. Likewise, there will be times when a functional format is best because listing accomplishments by major function will get attention quicker.

- Using the chronological format. The major blocks of information commonly found in a chronological format are:

  * Heading;
  * Objective statement;
  * Professional summary statement;
  * Professional experience listed in chronological order beginning with your most recent and moving backward until you've covered your entire work history;
  * Education/certifications; and
  * Related professional information.

- Using a functional format. The functional format organizes your work experience by major function, not chronologically. It's often used successfully when you're changing careers or professions.

- Marketing letters. Marketing letters succeed for four reasons: 1) they represent a more personal approach; 2) very few people use them; 3) they get face-to-face appointments when an opening doesn't exist; and 4) they are a way to expand your network list. The marketing letter is an expanded cover letter that emphasizes skills and achievements that are directly related to the needs of the organization.

7. Accomplishment/result statements:

- Key ingredient for your resume. Prepare accomplishment statements that accurately

NOTES

represent and describe your background. It's THE critical first step in your job search and in developing your resume database.

• Accomplishments statements are:

* More than a restated job description or summary of past responsibilities;

* Descriptions of specific professional and personal experiences; they describe completed projects, assignments, tasks; cross-functional teams you've lead or participated on; outcomes of your work or volunteer experiences;

* Specific descriptions of your skills, abilities and knowledge;

* Clues as to your talents and qualifications; and

* Short paragraphs that describe your "value" to someone who is interested in hiring you. The more you can describe how your background and experiences match the needs of the prospective employer, the greater your value is in the mind of that employer and the greater the chances are that the organization will want to call for an interview.

• Each accomplishment statement should include three parts:

* The action you took. Begin each statement with an action verb that describes what you did;

* The outcome or result of your action. Be sure to include a quantitative measure or number such as dollars saved, customer base increased, or revenue generated, etc.; and

* The scope of your work. This describes the project or task.

Chapter 5: Take charge of your selling tools II: Write letters that enhance your job search

1. Write letters to accompany your resume:

    *   Don't underestimate the power of a well - conceived and written cover letter. To write a powerful letter, start by thinking of it as the FIRST page of your resume. Remember, the person who screens resumes usually makes the first decision in 15 seconds, which includes time to scan your cover letter and connect with you.

    *   Write naturally and make sure you con- sider the five sections in all effective cover letters:

        *   Establish purpose including a WOW opening that grabs the reader's attention;
        *   Hold the reader's attention;
        *   Respond to a request for salary his- tory and requirements (if needed);
        *   Cover your follow-up and next steps; and
        *   Close.

    *   Thank-you notes and follow-up letters are as important to your job search as cover letters. Don't underestimate their power. Opportunities to use a thank-you or follow-up note are :

        *   After an informational interview;
        *   When you meet with a network contact;
        *   To summarize the results of a job interview and indicate your next steps in the hiring process;
        *   To thank that helpful administrative assistant or secretary who helped you when you arrived for a job inter- view; and
        *   When you receive a rejection letter.

NOTES

- Other types of notes:

  * Following up informational inter-
    views and meetings with your net-
    working contacts;
  * Following up job interviews: a thank
    you to the person who interviewed
    you;
  * Following up with an administrative
    assistant or secretary; and
  * Thank-you note when you don't
    receive an offer.

Chapter 6: Take charge of your inter-views

1. Five common types are the:

   - Screening interview;
   - Proposal interview;
   - Referral interview;
   - Information interview; and
   - Job interview.

2. Prepare for the first job interview. Three important tips when preparing for the interview:

   - Never assume the interviewer is prepared
     to interview you. Anticipate the inter-
     viewer won't be prepared and, in fact,
     may have thought about the interview
     only minutes before you arrived.
     Interviewers typically think of and ask
     questions off the top of their heads. They
     may be as uncomfortable and tense as
     you are.

   - Don't assume the interviewer will take
     sole responsibility for the interview. You
     must prepare yourself to participate,
     even guide, the interview in order to find
     out as much information as you can
     about the job and the employer's needs.
     Once you have identified job responsibil-
     ities and needs, you can discuss your

skills and accomplishments in terms of those needs. Employers want to find solutions to their problems. Your skills must offer that solution.

- Remember that interviewers evaluate and decide about you based not only on your knowledge and skills but also your:

  * Accomplishments and achievements;
  * Career and job goals;
  * Communication and relationship skills;
  * Ability to "fit" into the organization;
  * Appearance; and
  * Overall impression.

3. Guidelines for results-oriented interviewing:

- Your presentation:

  * Remember first impressions. You're making a significant impression on the interviewer during the first 30 seconds;
  * Convey impressions that often lead interviewers to reach subconscious conclusions – even before you speak; and
  * Be yourself; just be your BEST self.

- Your preparation:

  * Plan your drive time to arrive early – at least 30 minutes early. Waiting in the parking lot is better than getting stuck in traffic;
  * Dress consistently with the organization's and position's culture; be conservative;
  * Plan your attitude – positive attitude and body posture;
  * Talk about your skills and accomplishments and how they match the needs of the organization;

NOTES

* Anticipate the most often asked question: "Tell me about yourself" ; and

* Think of the interview as an exchange of information between two people. Answer each question with brief statements – don't use more than 90 to 100 seconds for each response.

• Listening skills:

* Prepare and be confident in your own material and presentation so you can actively attend (listen) to the interviewer;

* Listen for clues in what the interviewer says and in the voice inflection. Respond to those clues. Watch for clues in the non-verbal cues;

* Paraphrase what is said as a way of confirming what you've heard; and

* Prepare 10 to 15 questions, but remember, you may use only three or four.

• Your responses:

* Always respond positively and energetically;

* Never talk negatively about previous employers, no matter how bad the situation was;

* Focus all your responses on the job and the employer's needs, not on your needs and requests;

* Resist the urge to suggest solutions to problems discussed. Suggest how your experience makes it likely that you will help solve problems;

* Don't reject anything before it is offered or let negative reactions show. Keep an open mind; you can always say "no" later; and

* Send a thank-you note immediately after the interview. Prepare a separate thank-you note for the secretary or administrative assistant.

4. Plan for trait and behavioral questions:

    •   Trait questions are a structured way to assess your personality traits – organizational skills, flexibility, adaptability, energy and motivation, just to name a few. Trait questions relate more to characteristics of your personality than to your job skills;

    •   Behavior-based questions are open-ended questions to encourage you to describe a past action or achievement – how you handled a particular problem or a difficult person; and

    •   Know and plan for common interview questions – using your resume database. The information you provide helps the employer explore your present and past work history, what you've accomplished, and how you handled certain situations or solved problems. Sample questions fall into five general areas:

        *   Questions designed to screen you out;
        *   Other questions common to first interviews arranged into three categories:
            -   Professional experience;
            -   Managing and supervising experience; and
            -   Personal background.
        *   Two questions often used to end the first interview;
        *   Questions sometimes used for entry-level positions; and
        *   Questions you should have ready to ask during the interview.

5. Handling the first job interview:

    •   Survive the critical first 30 seconds and build rapport;

    •   Use small-talk to your benefit;

- Establish the time allowed for the interview;

- Begin the interview forcefully;

- Prepare and use a 2-1/2-minute drill;

- Attend to interviews in a positive way;

- Acknowledge the interviewer's message, by leaning slightly forward and responding;

- Take notes while listening;

- Ask questions to uncover needs and requirements;

- Describe your accomplishments; tell stories that directly relate to the interviewer's needs and requirements;

- Conclude the interview in a positive way – summarize;

- Identify next steps; and

- Send a follow-up letter.

6. Take charge of your second and subsequent interviews – guidelines:

- Scheduling your appointment;

- Preparing for individual interviews;

- Preparing for group interviews; and

- Sample interview questions you should ask during the second and subsequent interviews.

Chapter 7: Take charge of your negotiations

1. These ideas and techniques are meant to provide that little boost of confidence to competently negotiate a job offer that meets your personal and professional needs as well as those of the hiring organization.

2. What Is negotiation?: You and the employer must reach a mutual agreement, through discussion, on all terms of employment. And you must do so without damaging the relationship you've developed up to this point.

3. Evaluate the offer. Consider four critical areas:

    • Roles, responsibilities, expectations;

    • Resources available to you;

    • Rewards and outcomes or results; and

    • Obstacles – obvious and hidden.

4. As you negotiate, keep in mind these key points:

    • View negotiation as win - win;

    • Be clear about your needs;

    • Remember, everything is negotiable;

    • Know that you don't have to accept (or decline) the offer during negotiations;

    • Consider your needs for relocating;

    • Negotiate flexibly;

    • Clearly articulate your needs and requirements;

    • Negotiate benefits and incentives;

- Negotiate salary; and

- Finally, decide

5. Get the offer in writing.

6. Keep your job search moving while negotiating.

7. Employment contracts:

   - The environment that managers and administrators work in today means we must redefine the roles and responsibilities in health care organizations. Administrators succeed or fail by their ability to provide comprehensive, synergistic leadership; innovative management strategies; and significant investments in time.

   In this environment an employment contract can motivate positive changes. This legal document forms the organization's parameters for an administrator's authority, responsibility and accountability; it also commits the organizational support necessary to succeed. If one of these factors is limited or not clearly defined in formal employment contracts or informal agreements, success is possible but more difficult to achieve.